Fear No Art
You can do it!

Janette Benroth Reineke

WORKPLAY PUBLISHING

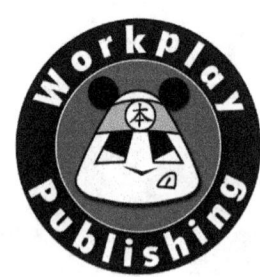

Published by Workplay Publishing
Newton, KS 67114
workplaypublishing.com

ISBN 0-9905545-3-8

Cover and interior design by Alison King
Interior photography by Janette Benroth Reineke

PRINTED IN THE UNITED STATES OF AMERICA

Dedication

In loving memory of my parents,
Eugene and Evelyn Benroth,
who always encouraged creativity;
and to my husband, children and families
for all their love and support.

Table of Contents

Preface

This art manual is an accumulation of my ideas, lesson plans and creative skills in teaching art to those residents who reside in assisted living or retirement facilities. It may also be a valuable guide for those working with children or adults with special needs or anyone interested in teaching an art lesson. Art has always been at the center of my very being. It surrounds me in every aspect of life. I believe that everyone has some kind of artistic ability whether it is having the eye to take an extraordinary photo or seeing something unusual in everything around us. Hasn't everyone seen images in the clouds?

I began my journey after I retired from teaching pre-school, kindergarten, first grade and elementary and junior high art in the public school system for 25 years. A few years before retiring, I began thinking about the elderly people with whom I've had the opportunity to interact, and how they had not had many opportunities to receive actual art lessons. Yes, they had many craft lessons, but I felt this was not a good way for them to be able to express themselves and to develop a sense of worth and self-esteem.

After much thought and deliberation, I volunteered to teach art lessons once a month at a local nursing home. We began by studying one artist a month and using that artist's technique in our lesson. It turned out to be such a success that I decided to expand to other facilities in the region. I decided to name my new career "Young at H'art by Janette," because people are never too old to be creative in the arts. I went into business as a roving art instructor on wheels (my car), charging a set fee which included all the supplies, the set up, a bulletin board display and the art lesson. The only thing the facility had to do was to encourage people to come to class.

At first it was difficult getting people to join the class. When they heard the words "art class" they were immediately intimidated. "I can't even draw a straight line," were the first words I usually heard from participants. But once they began attending classes, they found a side of themselves that they didn't know existed. They enjoyed expressing themselves and, as a result, gained confidence in their artistic abilities. They discovered that they COULD do it! Of course, they were not successful using every art medium, but they still learned new techniques, and they had to use their thinking skills to accomplish it. Everyone was successful in one way or another. There is no wrong way to practice art, and when they realized this, they became freer to express themselves without fear of being corrected. I constantly reminded them that Grandma Moses wasn't discovered until she was in her 70's. And look what happened to her!

With a little patience, lots of kind words and positive reinforcement, I found many talented people who were just waiting to be given the opportunity to create. I will never forget Pearl, who was 96 years old. She came to my art class and told me she had never had an opportunity to draw or do any kind of art. We were drawing a vase of flowers that day, a still life. With encouragement, she drew a beautiful picture using colored pencils. She looked at her picture when she finished and said with tears in her eyes, "Did I do that?"

Another time, a daughter of one resident who had been born deaf said, "What you did for my dad was invaluable." He looked forward to you coming and was so full of joy over his artwork. It's little moments like these that have made my teaching of seniors so rewarding.

One of the most important things you can do for someone is to encourage them, no matter their age. All of us have God-given talents to share and it just might be an artistic one.

So, fear no art! You CAN do it!

Artfully,

Janette Benrath Reineke

Preparation Rules & Class Procedure

1. Set up the tables and chairs in a u-shaped form with your easel in the opening of the u-shape and the sketch pad on it (*see photo at right*).

    This setup makes easy access for the instructor to walk around the inside of the u-shape and work with each person.

2. Make sure there is proper lighting for your students

3. Access to water and supplies is important

4. Establish a display area for the finished artwork

5. Using your large black marker, write (big enough for all to see) the name of the artist and their date of birth and death (e.g. "Jackson Pollock, 1912–1956"). If you are practicing a technique rather than studying an artist, write the technique on the sketch pad (e.g. "Primary and Secondary Colors).

6. Pass out all the required materials and place them in front of the space where each participant will be seated (*see photo at right*).

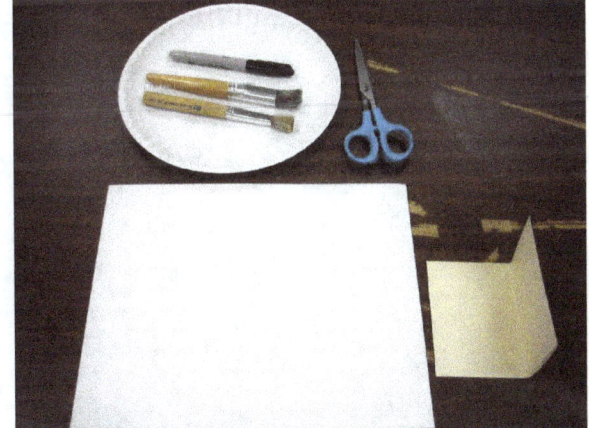

7. Begin playing the instrumental music CD. Keep *the volume low so the participants can hear your instructions.*

8. Welcome each person as they come into class. Place everyone where they can see the easel and hear you (*some can hear and see better than others so place them accordingly*).

9. It is not a good idea to show the participants your finished example. They are very intimidated and may think it looks too difficult for them to do. It is better to demonstrate just part of the procedure and then let them proceed.

10. Always compliment and give positive comments as they are working. Encourage them to do the best that they can. There are no mistakes in art. Everything is an expression of them.

11. Make sure all artwork is signed.

12. Always finish the class by displaying all of the day's artwork for the entire class to see.

13. Review the day's focus before the students leave to reinforce what they have accomplished.

14. Thank the class for coming and encourage them to return next time.

Sources for Art Supplies

1. C & S Supplies   1-800-288-9941

2. Hobby Lobby/Michael's

3. Dollar General

4. Good Will Industries

5. Walmart/Meijer/Target

6. Joanne Fabrics/any fabric supply stores

7. Thrift stores, garage sales and flea markets

8. Et Cetera Shops (MCC)

It's not the product, but the process that's important

General supplies needed for art classes

Tips *and* ***Tools*** *of the trade*

1. Tempera paints in all colors

2. Eight or more sets of watercolor paints – Prang or Crayola (single or double sets) If double, two people can share.

3. Good paint brushes: Small #4, Medium #6, and Large #10

4. Stenciling brushes

5. Water containers

6. Black sharpie markers

7. Roll of paper towels

8. Sketch pad (18" x 24")

9. Portable easel for sketch pad

10. Graphite pencils with erasers

11. Pencil and brush grippers (to help those with arthritus unable to grip)

12. Oil or chalk pastels

13. Masking tape

14. Large black marker for the instructor

15. Different colors of construction paper

16. White drawing paper (9" x 12") and light weight water color paper

17. Tag board

18. Q-tips

19. Good quality markers – all colors

20. Colored pencils

21. Four-ounce Elmer's glue bottles

22. Straight edges or rulers

23. Scissors (large enough for fingers to fit through)

24. Smocks or old shirts which can also be made from a garbage bag *(see above)*

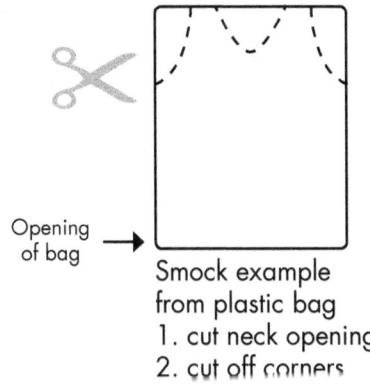

Opening of bag →

Smock example from plastic bag
1. cut neck opening
2. cut off corners

25. Bulletin board for display

26. Self hardening clay or firing clay if you have a kiln

27. Colored tissue

28. Old newspapers or plastic table covers

29. CD of instrumental "mood" music and a CD player

30. Collection of magazine pictures of flowers, butterflies and insects, animals, landscapes, etc.

You will need enough materials on hand to provide for each participant. If you have a limited budget, the participants can also share supplies.

I have found many of my supplies over the years at garage sales and flea markets for a very reasonable price.

*"[In art] there are no mistakes,
just happy accidents."
Bob Ross*

Jean (Hans) Arp
1887 – 1966

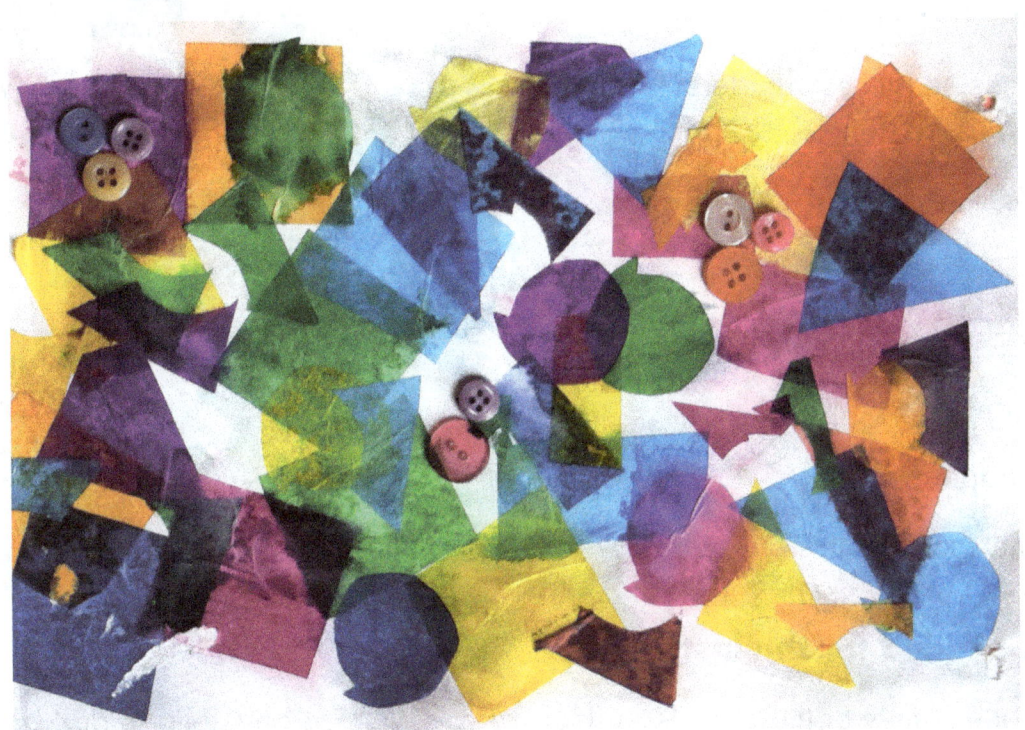

French Jean (Hans) Arp is associated with several art movements of the twentieth century. In 1911 he was influenced by the abstractions of Wassily Kandinsky (1866 – 1944). He was interested in the idea of spontaneous creativity of the human subconscious mind and this idea became dominant in his art. He created collages with torn paper, letting the pieces fall freely on a surface and then gluing them to the places where they landed.

Name of project: Collage

Collage (from the French: coller to glue) is a work of art, primarily the visual arts, made from assembling different forms to create a picture. In this lesson, we are using colored tissue pieces.

Objectives: to help the participants create a collage and to understand that "collage" is fun, easy and creative.

Getting started

Supplies needed for each person:

1. One cardboard piece 6" x 12" (preferably white)

2. Quarter size pieces of different colored tissue paper (15-20)

3. Elmer's glue bottle (4 oz)

4. Paint brush (#7 or larger)

5. Water pan

6. Paper towel

7. Small paper cup

8. A paint smock

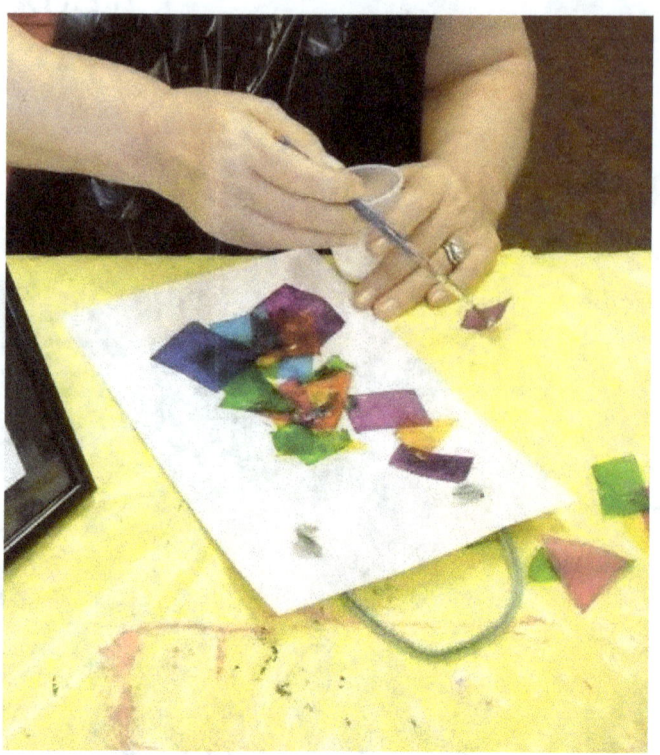

Supplies needed for the instructor:

1. A visual example of the artist Jean (Hans) Arp's work or any collage and a brief history of him *(see example)*

2. Floor easel with sketch pad

3. Black marker

4. Roll of masking tape for holding down the cardboard of people who only have use of one hand

5. A CD of instrumental music and CD player *(optional)*

Before the participants arrive, follow the preparation rules of the art lesson on page 9.

Freedom of expression is art at its finest

Lesson

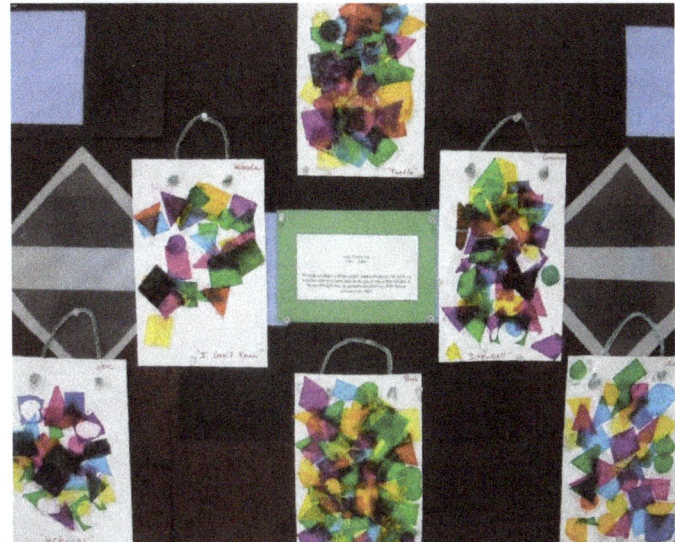

1. Introduce the artist and show an example of his work. Explain what a collage is and show examples of one.

2. Demonstrate how to mix the Elmer's glue solution. Put one quarter size drop of glue in the paper cup and mix, using #7 paint brush with just enough water to cover the glue. Mix thoroughly. It should not be too thick.

3. Demonstrate how to apply the glue solution to the cardboard with your brush. Only cover a small section at a time.

4. Drop each piece of colored tissue onto the glue covered cardboard in a random fashion. Paint down each piece with the solution. When finished, cover the whole board of tissue pieces with the glue solution using the paint brush.

5. Tell the class to think of names for their collages. The name can be any word or words and it doesn't have to convey meaning or any interpretation of their artwork (e.g. "Craziness," "Jonestown," or "Buttercup").

6. After the collages dry, use the black marker to write the each person's name and the title of their collage at the bottom of the cardboard.

7. Have each participant present their collage and explain why they named it the way they did. Give positive comments whenever possible.

8. Review the name of the artist and inform the class they have made collages just like the famous artist Hans Arp.

9. Display the finished art work and a brief paragraph about the artist Jean (Hans) Arp on a bulletin board where everyone can see it *(see example)*.

Bulletin Board Header

Duplicate page for multiple uses

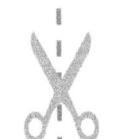

Jean (Hans) Arp 1887-1966

He created collages with torn paper, letting the pieces fall freely on a surface and then gluing them down where they fell. He saw this as spontaneous creativity of the human subconscious mind.

Paul Cezanne
1839 – 1906

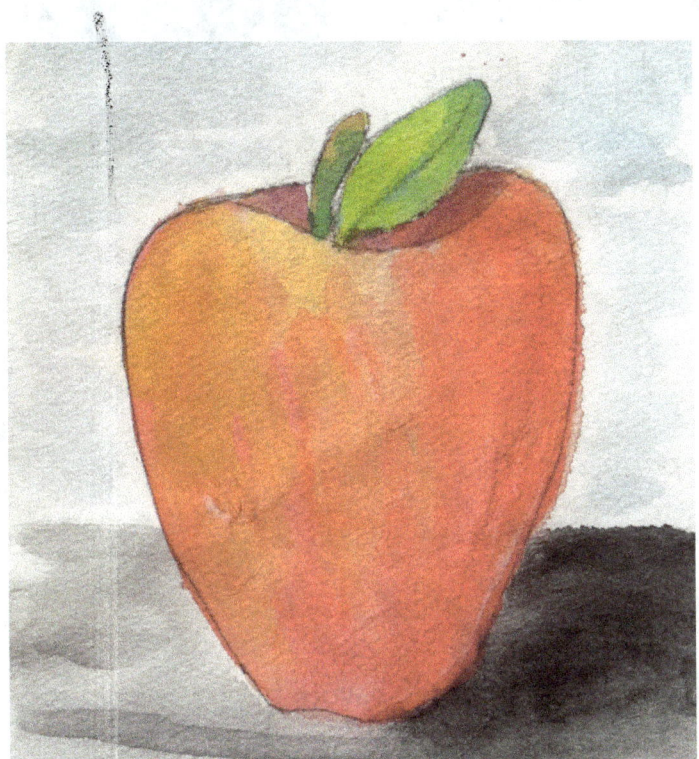

Cezanne, sometimes called the father of modern painting, was one of the greatest post *impressionistic* painters of all time. He was a very shy man, but had many famous artist friends like fellow painter Camille Pissarro.

He usually painted *still lifes*, or pictures of objects that do not move. Vases, fabrics and fruits were arranged in his studio as the subjects of many of his paintings.

Name of project: *Still life*—pictures of objects that do not move.

Objective: to create a still life of an apple.

Words in itallics can be found in the Art Terminology Dictionary

Getting started

Supplies needed for each participant:

1. 4" x 6" piece of watercolor paper

2. 5" x 7" piece of black paper (for the background)

3. Watercolor paint set with brush

4. Water pan

5. Paper towel

6. Pencil

7. Apple pattern *(see page 25)*

8. Plastic or real apple

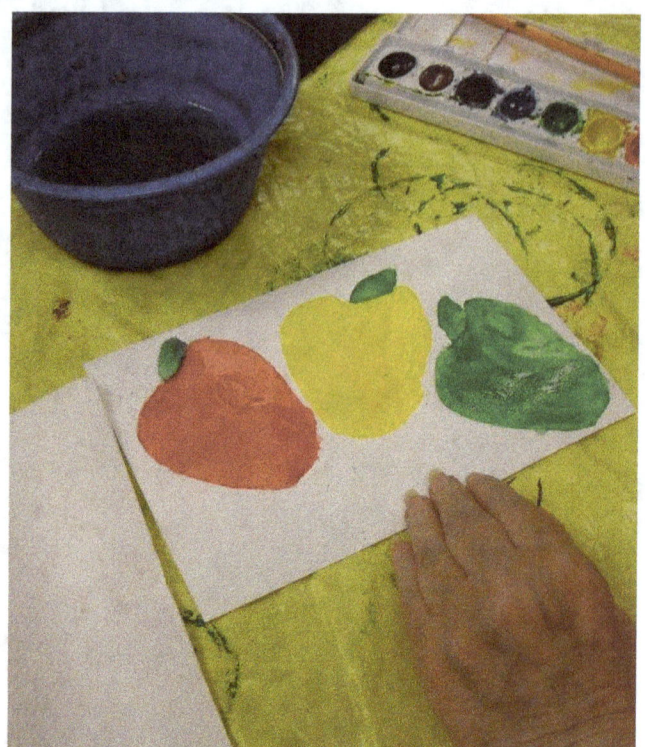

Supplies needed for instructor:

1. A visual example of the artist Cezanne's work and a brief history of him.

2. Floor easel with sketch pad

3. Black marker

4. 4" x 6" piece of water color paper

5. Water color paint set with brush

6. Pan of water

7. Apple pattern

8. Plastic or real apple

9. Roll of masking tape

10. A CD of instrumental music and CD Player (optional)

Before the participants arrive, follow the preparation rules of the art lesson on page 9.

Lesson

1. Introduce the artist Cezanne by reading a brief history of him.

2. Show an example of his work and other examples of *still lifes.*

3. Explain the meaning of a *still life (see dictionary of terms).*

4. Show the participants how to lightly trace their apple pattern with a pencil about ¾ of the way down on their water color paper.

5. Show how to draw the *horizon line* (¾ down the page) behind their apple pattern *(see diagram A below.)*

6. Explain how to use their water color paint set, wetting their brush first and then dipping their brush in the red paint.

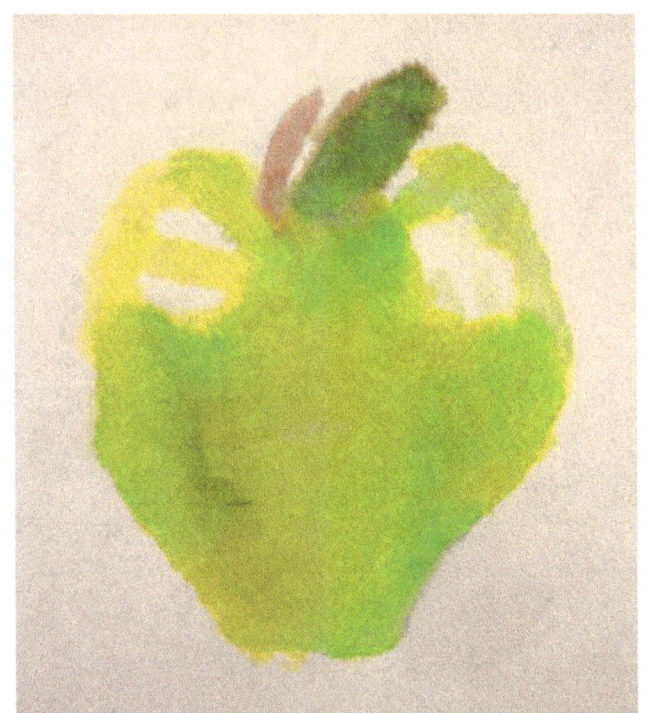

7. Show them how to paint one side of their apple darker than the other side by using more paint on their brush.

8. The other side of the apple will be lighter, showing where the source of light is coming from. A lighter red can be made by using more water that paint. You can also lighten the apple color by adding a hint of yellow or orange.

9. Have them paint the stem brown and the leaf green.

10. Paint the surface under the apple a color of their choice (not red).

11. Show the participant's work when they are finished and glue them to the black background piece.

12. Display for all to see.

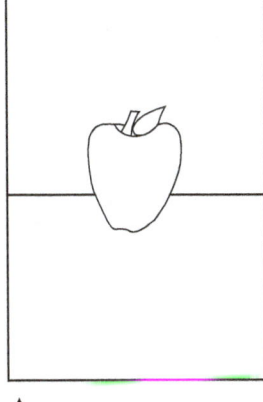

A

Use with Paul Cezanne lesson

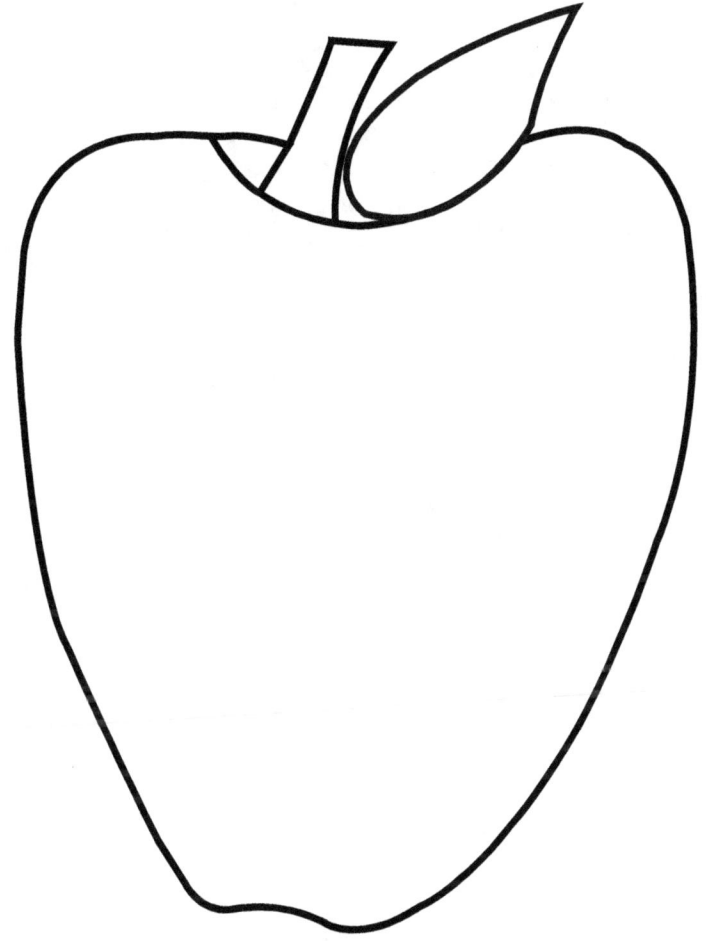

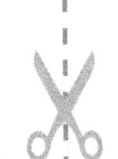

Paul Cezanne   1839-1906

Paul Cezanne painted *still lifes*, pictures of objects that do not move, like vases, fruits and fabrics that he arranged for display in his studio. He is often called the "father of modern painting."

M.C. Escher
1898-1972

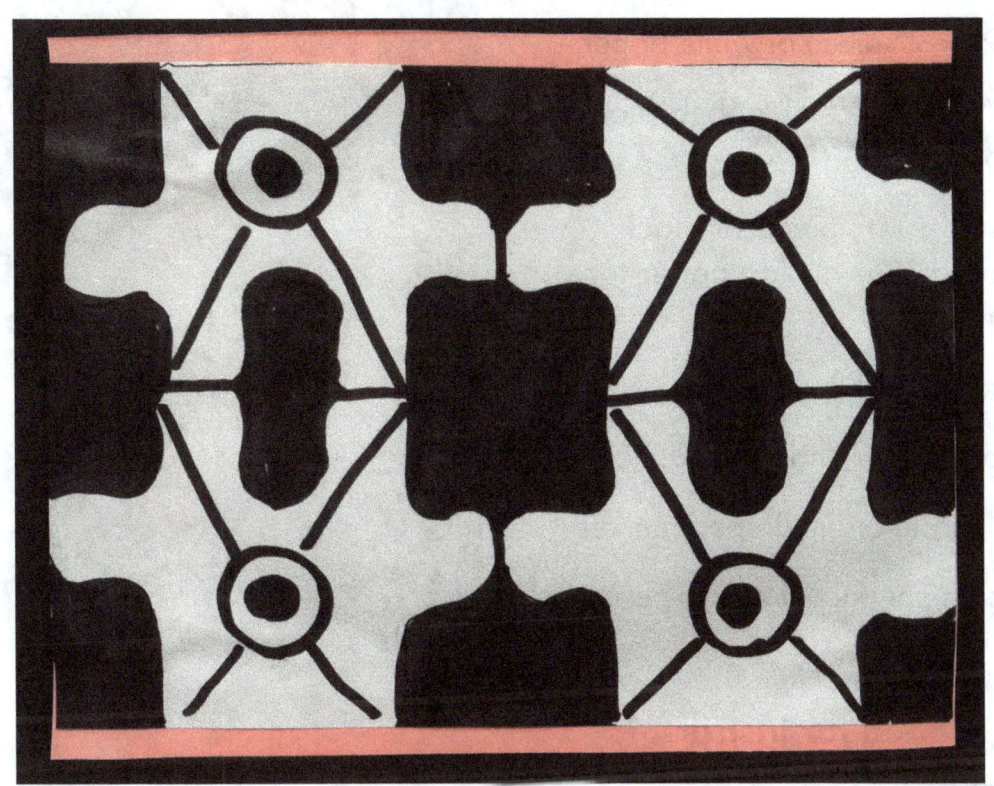

   M.C. Escher is one of the world's most famous *graphic* artists. He is most famous for his so-called impossible structures such as his *"Sky and Water"* series. He created *optical illusions* which suggest three dimensions rather than two by repeating a shape over and over again (*tessellation*).

Name of project: *Optical Illusion and tessellations.* An *optical illusion* is a visual experience that includes some kind of false perspective of what is actually there—something designed deliberately to fool the eye. A *tessellation* is created when a shape is repeated over and over again, covering an area without any gaps or overlaps.

Objective: to create an optical illusion by repeating a design over and over again.

Getting started

Supplies needed for each participant:

1. One 9" x 9" piece of white paper

2. One 3" x 3" piece of tagboard or thin cardboard

3. One 10" x 10" piece of black or colored construction paper for background

4. Scissors

5. Black or colored wide tipped marker

6. Black sharpie or fine tipped marker

7. Newspaper or paper towel to put under white paper

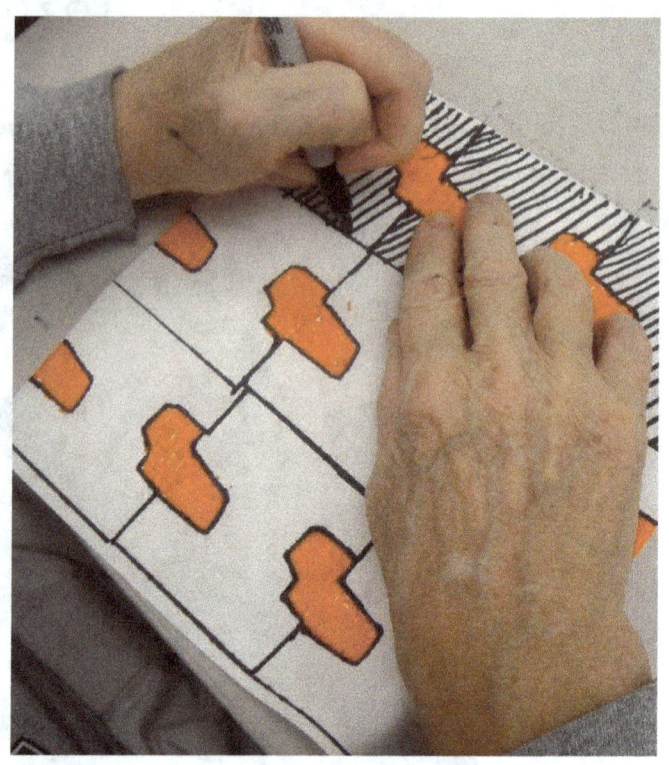

Supplies needed for instructor:

1. A visual example showing an optical illusion or one of M.C. Escher's works, such as *"Sky and Water I"*

2. Floor easel with sketch pad

3. Large black marker

4. Roll of masking tape for holding down student's work *(if needed)*

5. A CD of instrumental music and CD player *(optional)*

Before the participants arrive, follow the preparation rules of the art lesson on page 9.

"[In art] there are no mistakes, just happy accidents."
Bob Ross

Lesson

1. Introduce the artist and show an example of an optical illusion either M.C Escher's or your own *(see illustration)*.

2. Ask the participants what they see in the optical illusion.

3. Explain that not everyone sees the same thing(s).

4. Picking up the 3" x 3" piece of tagboard, show the students how to cut out two free form shapes from two sides of the tagboard, leaving all four corners in tact (see illustration on page 30).

5. Place the new shape that is left after the cuttings at the top of the 9" x 9" piece of white paper aligning the corners.

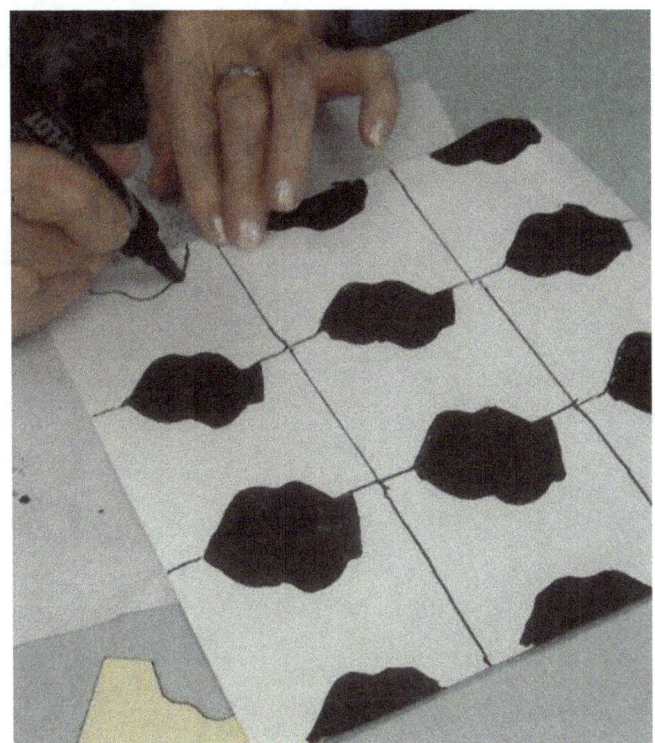

6. Trace the tagboard shape nine times with the black sharpie which will fill the 9" x 9" paper. Make sure there are no overlaps when tracing.

7. With a black or colored marker, fill in the *negative spaces* (see picture above).

8. Glue the finished paper onto the colored background by putting glue in each corner on the back.

9. Have each student give a title to their optical illusion.

10. Go around the room and have each person show their optical illusion and tell their title to the class. Discuss images that have been created.

11. Review the name of the artist and tell the class that they have created an optical illusion by repeating one shape over and over (*tessellation*)

12. Display the finished art work and a brief paragraph about the artist M.C. Escher on a bulletin board where everyone can see it.

Resources: Project Patterns

Use with M.C. Escher lesson

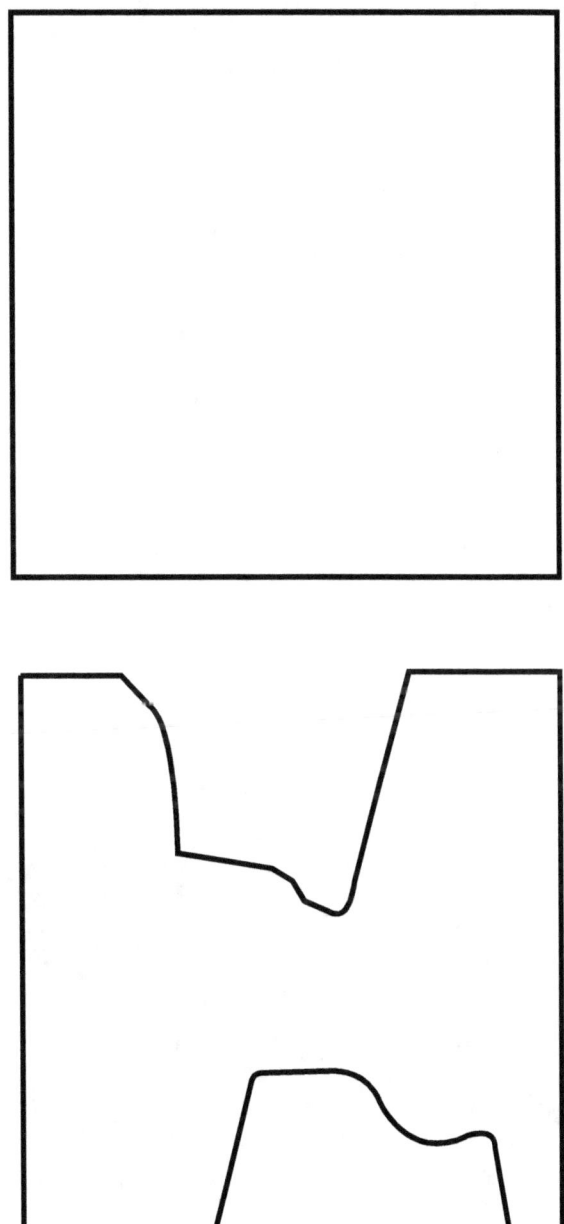

Duplicate page for multiple uses

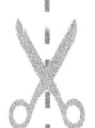

M.C. Escher 1898-1972

M.C. Escher is known for optical illusions: visual experiences in which there is some kind of false perspective of what is actually there—something designed deliberately to fool the eye.

Piet Mondrian
1872 – 1944

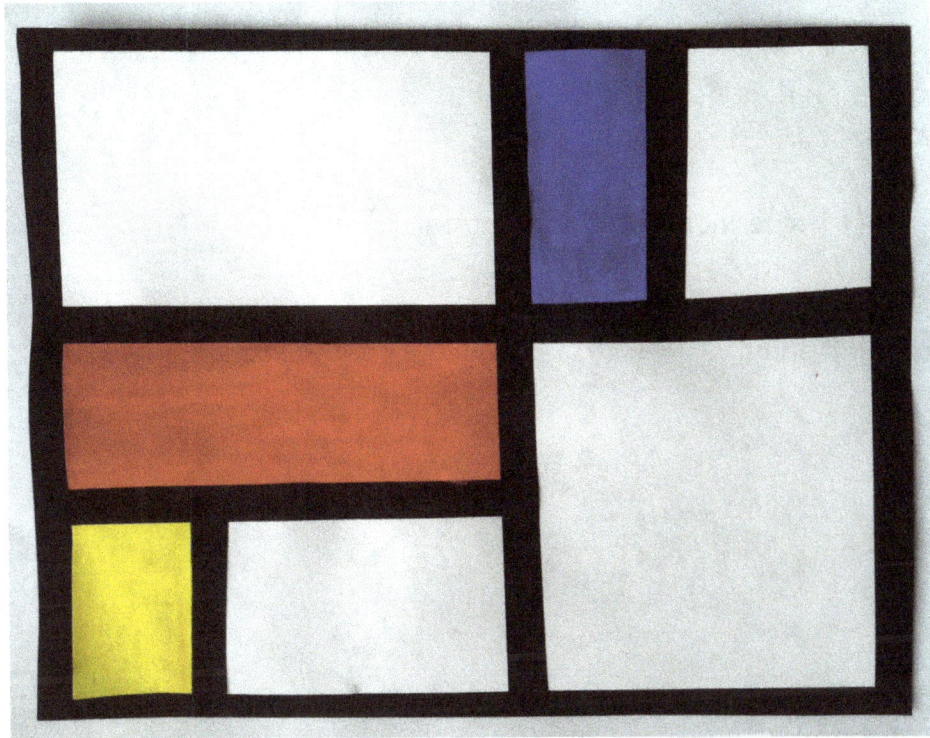

Piet Mondrian was born in Holland. He studied to be an artist after completing his regular schooling. After 1910, he began to paint abstract designs instead of real life people and landscapes. He wanted to create pictures that expressed thoughts and feelings with perfect harmony between lines and colors. He worked hard to find just the right placement of lines which made squares and rectangles.

Name of project: *A "Mondrian" abstract painting*

Objective: to create an *abstract* design using the painting style of Mondrian

Getting started

Supplies needed for each participant:

1. 8" x 11" piece of heavy white paper
2. 9" x 12" piece of black construction paper (background)
3. Black Sharpie marker
4. Ruler
5. 3 or 4 strips (11 x ½ inches) of black paper
6. Paint brush
7. Paper plate (for paint)
8. Water pan
9. Elmer's glue
10. Scissors
11. Art smock

Supplies needed for instructor:

1. A visual example of Mondrian's work and a brief history of him
2. Floor easel with sketch pad
3. Large black marker
4. Roll of masking tape
5. Bottles of red, yellow and blue tempera paint
6. Strips of one half inch black paper
7. Scissors
8. Paint brush
9. Elmer's glue
10. CD of instrumental music and CD player (optional)
11. art smock

Before the participants arrive, follow the preparation rules of the art lesson on page 9.

Lesson

1. Introduce the artist by reading a brief biography and showing examples of his work.

2. On the easel pad, show how to divide the white paper into sections of squares or rectangles (no more than six sections) with the ruler and black marker.

3. Using the three *tempera* colors, give each participant a large "puddle" of red, yellow and blue paint. Instruct them to paint each section a different color, leaving a few plain white.

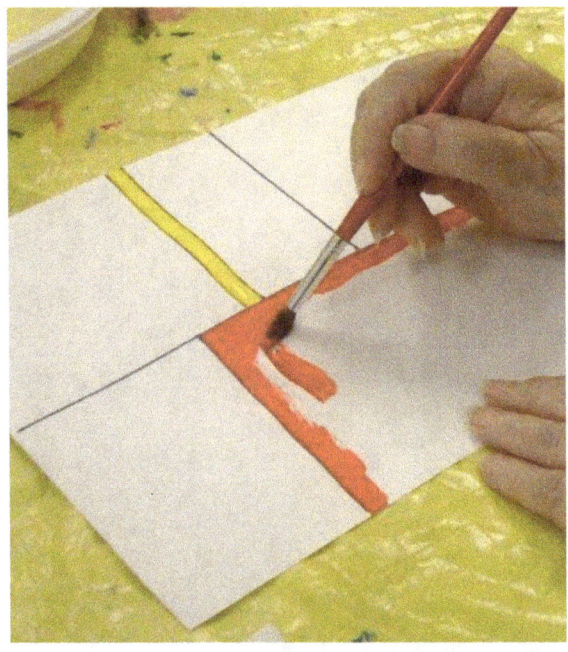

4. When they are finished, help them glue their black strips over the black marker lines. Put the glue on the painted paper instead of the strips makes gluing much easier and tidier.

5. Glue their finished design onto the black construction paper

6. Have the participant's title their work

7. Show everyone's finished projects and mount them on the bulletin board for all to see.

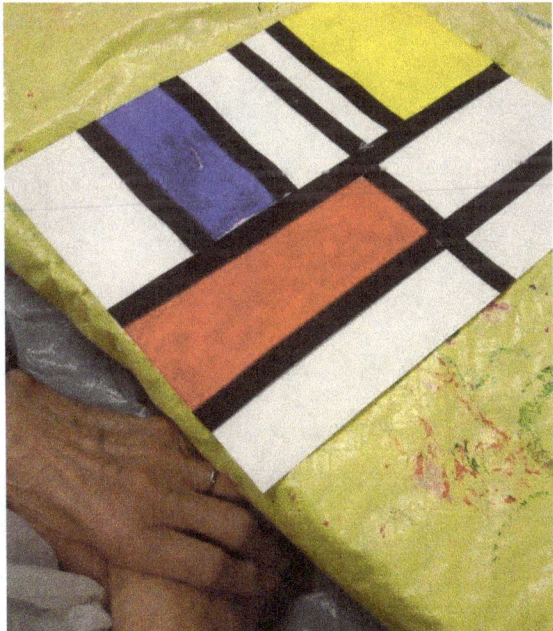

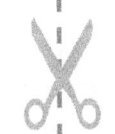

Piet Mondrian 1872-1944

Mondrian wanted to create a design that expressed perfect harmony between lines and color. He was famous for abstract images which did not have any particular subject or name. His most famous paintings are made entirely of straight lines and simple colors.

Claude Monet
1840-1926

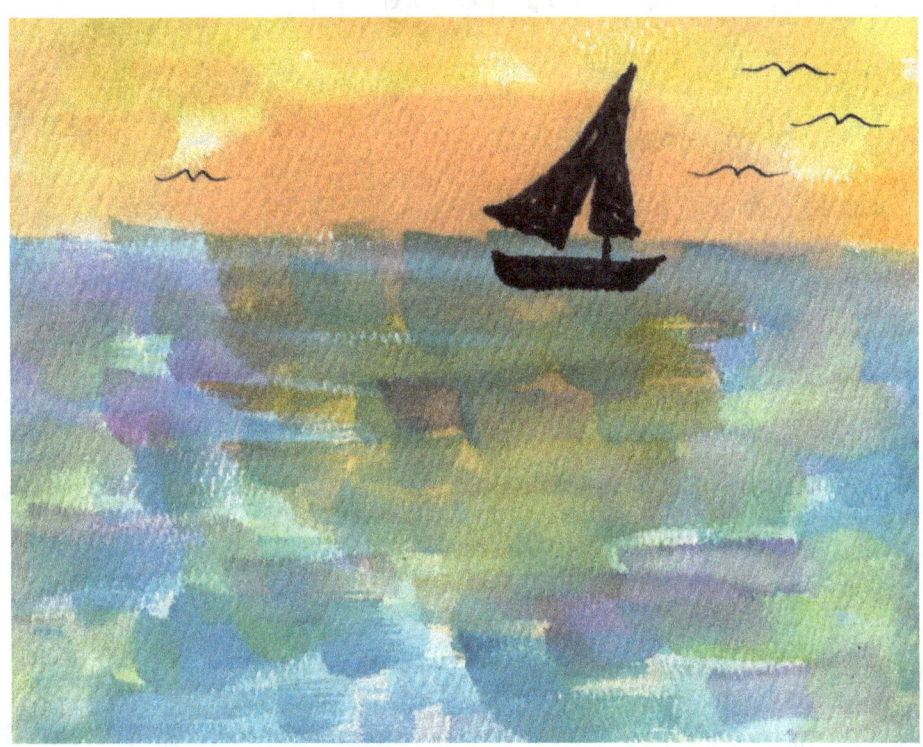

Claude Monet (mo-NAY) was a French painter who is best known as the leader of the Impressionists, a group of painters who painted what they saw and felt rather than painting something exactly the way it looked. Monet was known for painting with short brush strokes and dabbles and splashes of pretty colors, catching light and reflection in his work. From a distance, his paintings gave the *impression* of an idea because of the way the colors blended together (e.g. "Terrace at St. Adresse").

Name of project: *Watercolor seascape painting*

Objectives:
- to create a *seascape* painting using the impressionistic style of Monet
- to instruct participants to use watercolors successfully
- to develop a sense of accomplishment
- to appreciate the style and technique of Claude Monet

Getting started

Supplies needed for each participant:

1. A set of 8 or 16 watercolors (Prang or Crayola)

2. Paint brush (included in watercolor set)

3. 4" x 6" piece of watercolor paper

4. Black Sharpie marker

5. Container to hold water for rinsing brush

6. Paper towel

7. 5" x 7" colored construction paper for the background (orange, yellow, green or blue)

8. Piece of white scrap paper

9. Paint smock

Supplies needed for instructor:

1. A visual example of Monet's work and a short history of him (e.g. "Terrace at Sainte-Adresse")

2. Floor easel with sketch pad

3. Black Sharpie marker

4. Roll of masking tape for holding down the paper of those who need it for stability.

5. CD of instrumental music and CD player (optional)

6. A picture of a small sailboat or a model

Before the participants arrive, follow the preparation rules of the art lesson on page 9.

Lesson

1. Introduce the artist by reading a brief biography and showing examples of his work.

2. Explain water coloring and how to use the watercolor paints

3. Show how to do the short, quick brush stroke method of impressionistic painting.

4. Explain what the horizon line is and show an example of one from one of Monet's paintings.

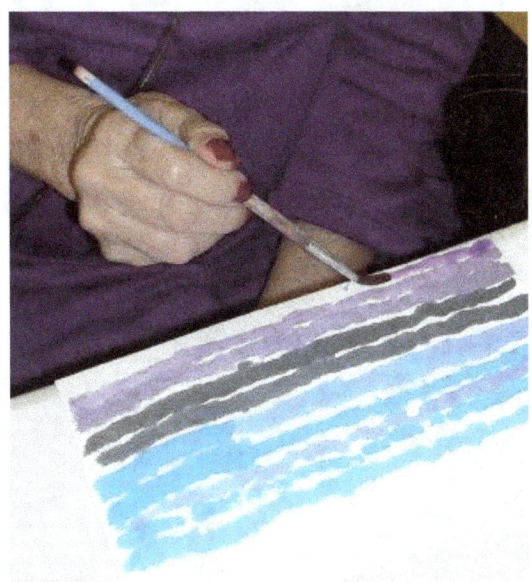

5. Have each participant paint a wavy line down about one and one half inches from the top of their water color paper (placed horizontally) to represent the horizon line.

6. Using the short quick brush stroke method, have the participants fill in the space below the horizon line with cool colors (blue, green and purple) to represent the ocean. Tell them to leave a few white spaces open to represent the caps of the waves.

7. Above the horizon line, using the short quick brush stroke method, have participants use the warm colors (red, yellow and orange) to represent the colors of the sunset. Note: it's best to paint in order from light to dark. Use yellow first, then orange followed by red.

8. While their paintings are drying, show participants how to make a simple sailboat after showing them the picture of one or the model (*two triangles with a half circle beneath them*). Have them practice first on the piece of scrap paper using the black marker.

9. After practicing drawing a small sailboat in *proportion*, have them use the black marker and draw it on their dry water color painting. Make sure the sails of the boat overlap the sunset and the boat's hull is in the water. Make sure they fill the boat in solidly with the black marker so the sail boat looks like a silhouette.

10. Mount their paintings on colored construction paper that enhances one of the colors in each painting.

11. Write their names under the appropriate paintings.

12. Show all the watercolor paintings to the class.

13. Give positive comments and review the name of the artist and his style.

14. Display the paintings on a bulletin board for all to see.

Claude Monet

45

Duplicate page for multiple uses

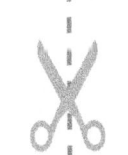

Claude Monet   1840-1926

Monet (MO-NAY) painted with short brush strokes and dabbles and splashes of pretty colors. He was the leader of the Impressionists, painters who painted what they saw and felt rather than painting something exactly the way it looked.

Louise Nevelson
1900 – 1988

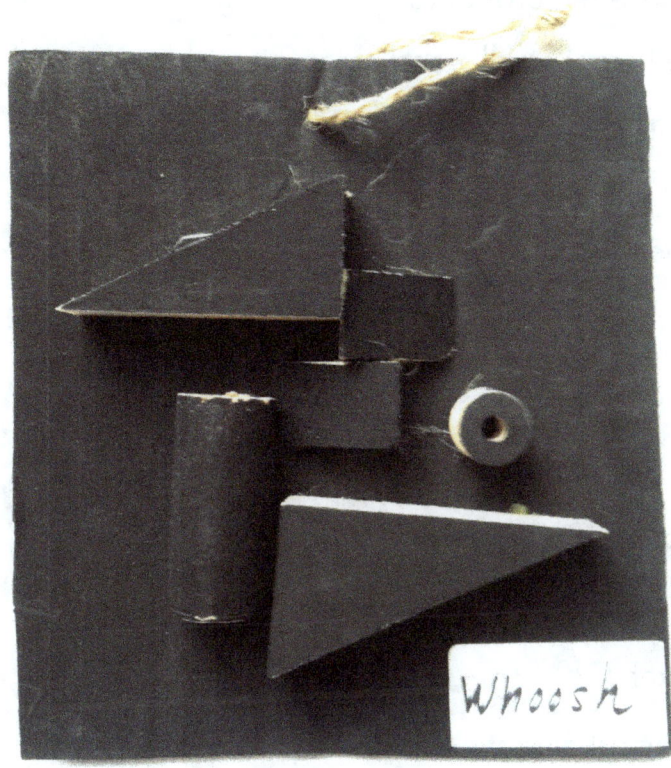

   Louise Nevelson is known for her *assemblages* made from found objects and gluing then onto cardboard or into a box. As a child Louise had access to wonderful scraps of wood because her father owned a lumberyard. She created *assemblages* or art created from odds and ends of wood and other things she found. Her sculptures appear puzzle like, with multiple cut pieces placed into wall sculptures or independently standing. She became famous for this unique style of sculpture.

Name of project: *Wood collage.* A collage is made from different forms to create a picture. In this lesson, we are using wood scraps.

Objective: to create an *abstract* (unrecognizable) or *realistic* (recognizable) *collage* using wood scraps

Getting started

Supplies needed for each participant:

1. 8" x 8" heavy piece of cardboard
2. Seven or more different small wood scrap pieces
3. Black tempera paint
4. Paint brush (#10 or similar)
5. Small paper plate
6. Paper towel
7. Art smock

Supplies needed for instructor:

1. Visual example of Louise Nevelson's work
2. Floor easel with sketch pad
3. Large black marker
4. Glue gun with several glue sticks for teacher use only
5. Large assortment of small scraps of wood
6. Black tempera paint
7. White marker or white labels for the title of the work
8. 8" x 8" piece of cardboard
9. Tool for puncturing a hole in the carboard (auger)
10. Pieces of cord or string for hanging finished projects
11. Paint brush
12. Paper plate
13. Art smock
14. CD of instrumental music and CD player (optional)

Before the participants arrive, follow the preparation rules of the art lesson on page 9.

Lesson

1. Introduce the artist by reading a short history of the artist Louise Nevelson.

2. Explain the definition of *collage*

3. Have everyone paint their cardboard black using the blob of paint that you have squeezed out for them on their paper plate. (Place paper towel underneath cardboard) Let it dry.

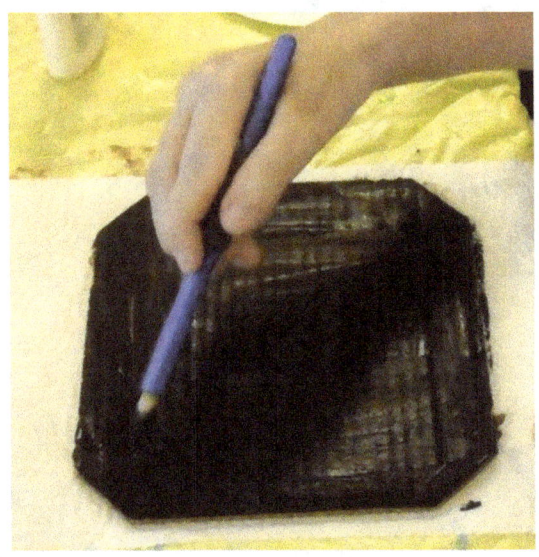

4. Choosing seven or more pieces of wood, demonstrate how to place their pieces of wood onto the painted black cardboard to create a *collage*. It can be *realistic* or *abstract*.

5. After completing your demo and gluing it down on your black cardboard with the glue gun, invite the class to begin assembling their *collage*.

6. When they have completed their *collages*, glue each one down for them with your glue gun and use an auger or other tool to punch holes in the cardboard for hanging. Have each participant title their *collage*

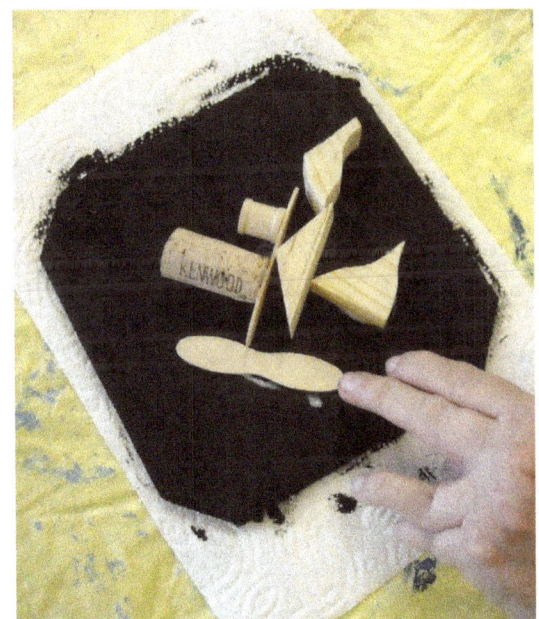

7. Show the finished *collages* to everyone

8. Review the name of the artist and display for all to see.

Bulletin Board Header

Duplicate page for multiple uses

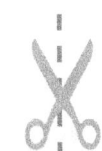

Louise Nevelson 1900-1988

Nevelson is known for her assemblages—gluing scraps of wood onto cardboard or into a wooden box. Coating it with one color of paint gives the shape a texture that brings out the design of the assemblage and disguises the parts and pieces.

Georgia O'Keeffe
1887 – 1986

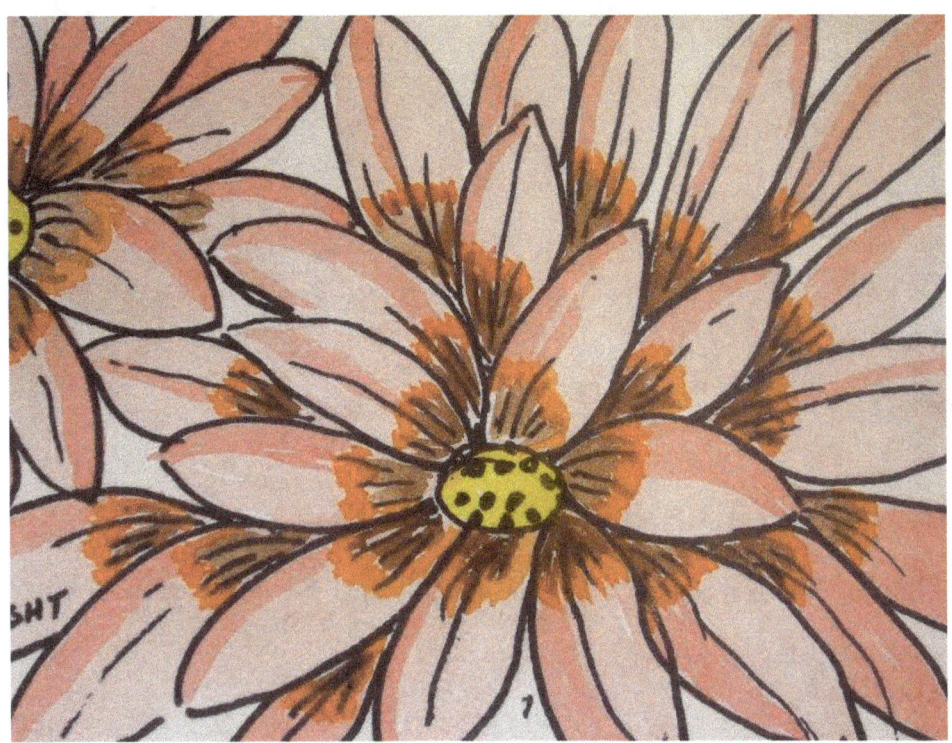

Georgia O'Keeffe, an American painter, is known for her paintings of flowers that fill the canvas. She often painted the flowers' tips going right off the edge. Sometimes she would paint only a part of the flower so close up that you would feel like you were looking deep inside (e.g. *"Oriental Poppies"*).

Name of project: *Watercolor flowers*

Objective: to create a large flower, Georgia O'Keeffe style, using watercolor as the medium

Getting started

Supplies needed for each participant:

1. 5" x 6½" piece of watercolor paper

2. Watercolors

3. Brush (#7 or larger)

4. Black Sharpie marker

5. Paper towel

6. Water pan

7. Art smock (optional)

Supplies needed for instructor:

1. A visual example of Georgia O'Keeffe's work and a brief history of her.

2. Floor easel with sketch pad

3. Large black marker

4. 5" x 6½" piece of water color paper

5. Paint brush

6. Water colors

7. Colored background paper for finished flower

8. Glue

9. Pan of water

10. Roll of masking tape

11. CD of instrumental music and CD player (optional)

12. Pictures of large flowers

Before the participants arrive, follow the preparation rules of the art lesson on page 9.

Lesson

1. Introduce the artist and show and example(s) of her work.

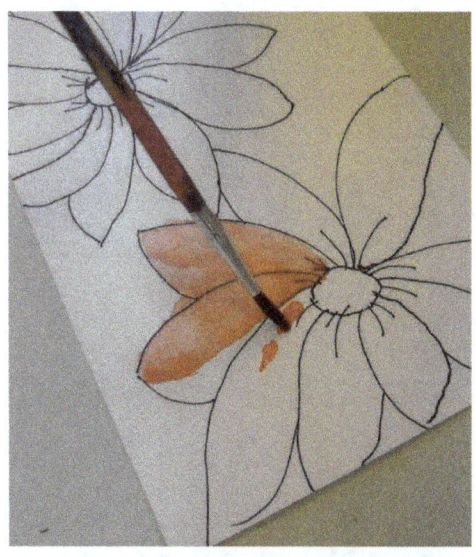

2. Lay out pictures of flowers on the tables for students to look at.

3. Emphasize that Georgia O'Keeffe painted large flowers so that people would appreciate their beauty. There will be only two rules today. The flowers have to be large and part of the flower has to go off the paper.

4. Using the black marker, show the student's how to make a circle the size of a quarter on their w.c. paper, preferably not in the middle of the paper. This circle is the center of the flower.

5. After drawing the circle, show the student's how to make one petal extending from the quarter-sized circle.

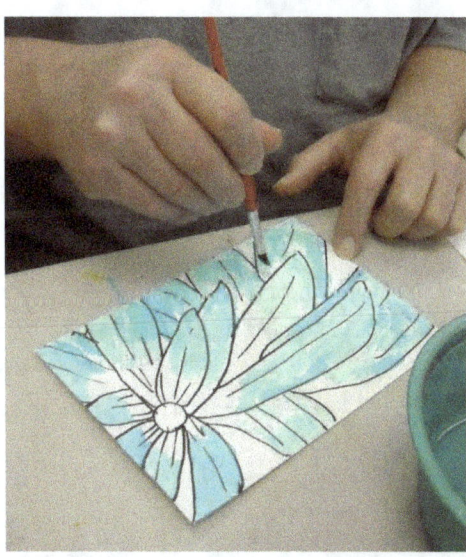

6. Continue adding petals until the petals are surrounding the circle. Keep reminding the students that their flowers should be big and part of it has to go off the paper. Keep adding petals until the paper is filled.

7. Show the students how to use the water colors to paint their flowers emphasizing that they can be more than one color.

8. When finished, if they wish, they can add lines with their black marker to their flowers to show details.

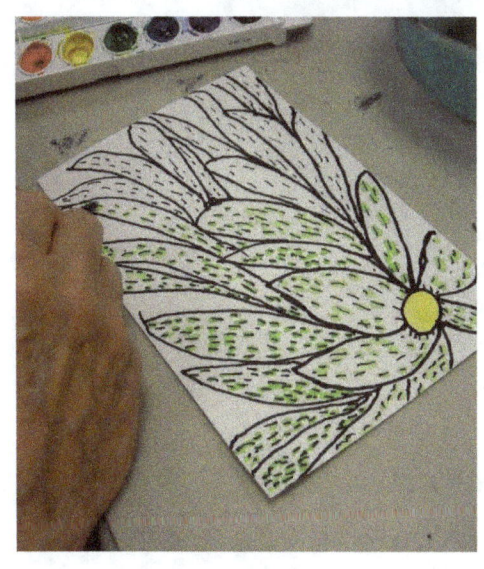

9. Choose a background paper color that is the same color as the painted flowers and glue their painting to the colored paper

10. Have students sign their names along the edge of a flower petal.

11. Hold up each student's finished work, praising them and their accomplishments.

12. Display the finished paintings for all to see.

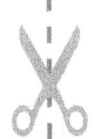

Georgia O'Keeffe   1887-1986

Georgia O'Keeffe, an American painter, is known for her paintings of flowers that fill the canvas. Often she painted the flowers' tips going right off the edge. Sometimes she would paint only a part of the flower so close up that you would feel like you were looking deep inside.

Jackson Pollock
1912 – 1956

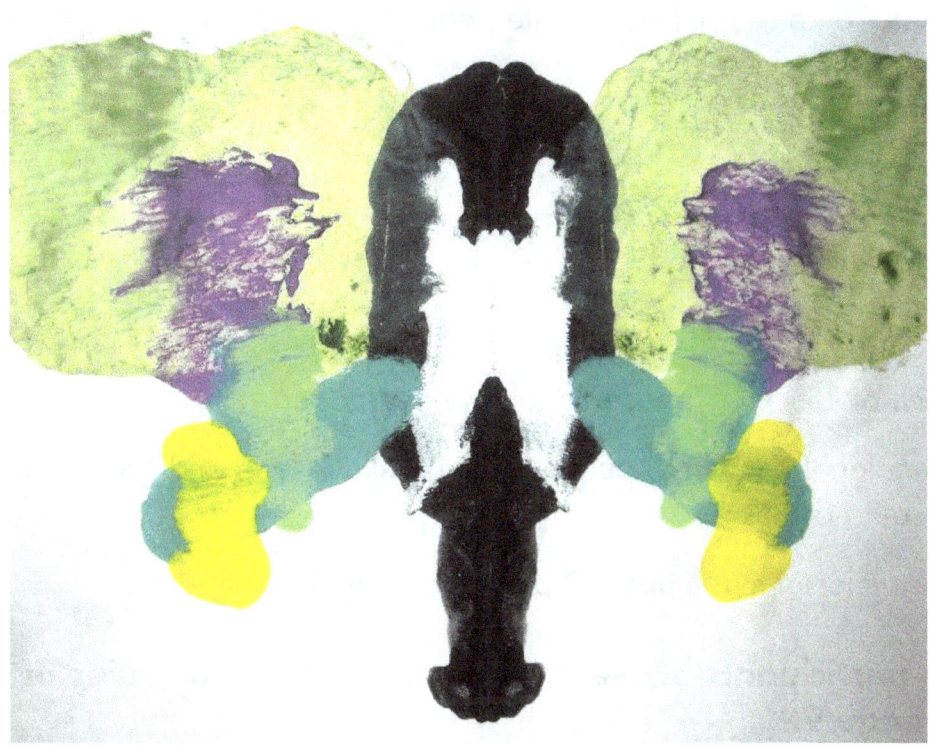

Jackson Pollock was an American painter who experimented in painting techniques to create an abstract style. He used his entire body in the painting process thus defining the term *"action painting."* He would place his canvas on the floor and as he rapidly walked around it, he dipped his brush into the paint can throwing the paint directly from the paint can onto the canvas. His wild designs sometimes incorporated other surprise elements such as his own handprints or some of his own personal possessions. All of his experiments demonstrate variety of shape, line and color that are found in abstract painting.

Name of project: Abstract *blob* design

Objective: to imitate Pollock's abstract style of painting using the folded method of painting with different colors *blobs* of paint

Getting started

Supplies needed for each participant:

1. One 11" x 16" piece of heavy white paper

2. Art smock or apron

Supplies needed for instructor:

1. Floor easel with sketch pad

2. Fine-tipped black marker

3. One piece of 11" x 16" piece of heavy white paper

4. Different colors (black, red, purple, green, yellow, blue and green) of tempera paint in squirt bottles.

5. CD of instrumental music and CD player (optional)

Before the participants arrive, follow the preparation rules of the art lesson on page 9.

*Freedom of expression
is art at its finest*

Lesson

1. Introduce the artist and show an example of his work.

2. Using a piece of 11" x 16" piece of white construction paper, demonstrate folding the paper in half width-wise.

3. Squeeze a *blob* of one of the tempera colors on one side of your folded paper.

4. Close the paper and rub the outside of the paper with the pads of your fingers. By doing this you will transfer that color onto the opposite side of the paper.

5. Open up the paper and show the class what has happened. Discuss what they see, using the word "symmetry"—one half of something is exactly like the other side of design.

6. Repeat this process 5 more times with the remaining colors of tempera paint onto your paper.

7. Now have the class fold their papers in half and re-open them.

8. The instructor will walk around the class and squeeze a *blob* of paint onto one side of each participant's folded paper.

9. The participants will close their folded papers and rub on the outside with their fingers.

10. Repeat this procedure until all six colors of paint have been used.

11. Discuss what has been created. They may see butterflies, animals or anything using their imagination. Have each participant title their abstract *blob* design and write it (or you do it for them) on the bottom of their paper with a black small tipped small tipped marker.

12. Display the finished abstracts on the bulletin board for all to see.

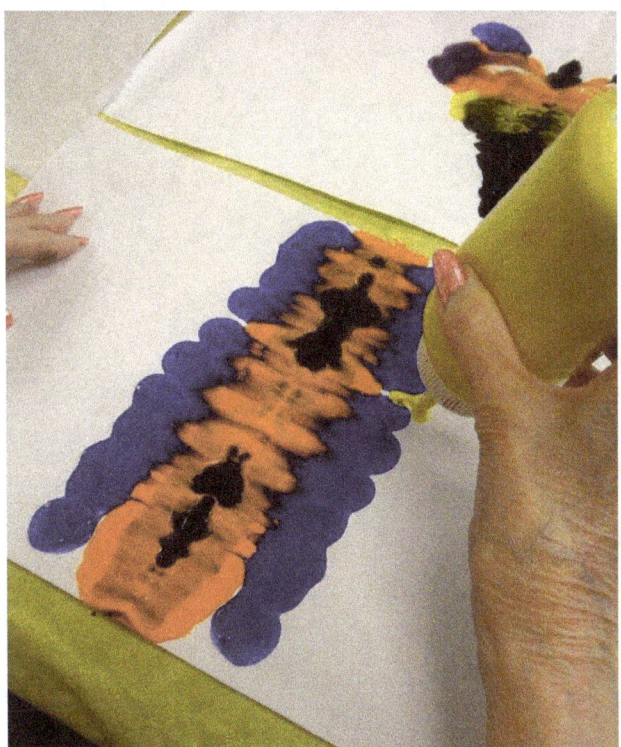

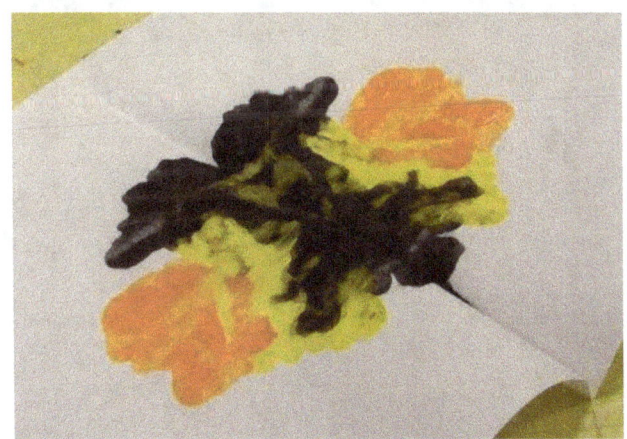

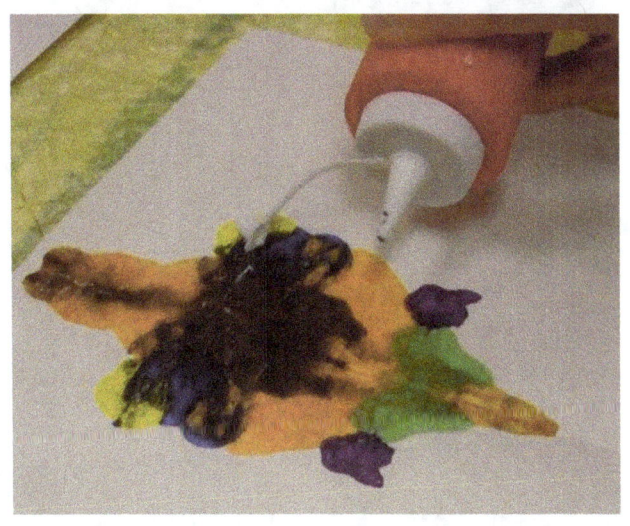

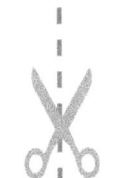

Jackson Pollock   1912-1956

Jackson Pollock wanted his paintings to be different so he created "action" paintings which included throwing and spattering paint. Our creations were done by placing paint "blobs" on one half of a folded piece of paper, closing it and then opening it, creating a symmetrical image.

Rembrandt Harmensz van Rijh
1606 – 1669

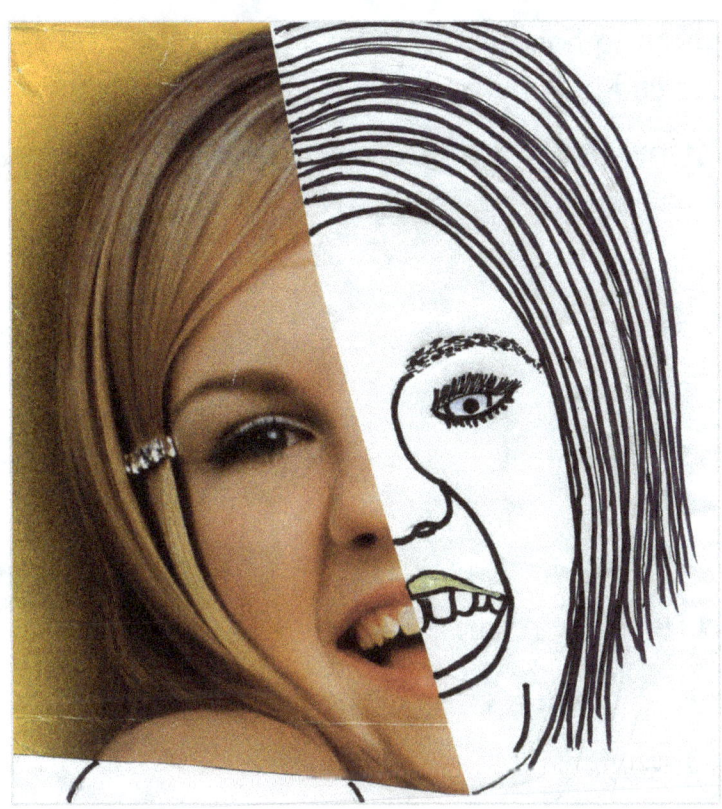

Born in Holland in 1606, Rembrandt is one of the few artists in history who has been known by his first name. His fame has grown over the years, and his paintings and drawings are priceless.

By looking in a mirror, he painted and drew many self portraits. He also painted many portraits of his family members. He liked to use strong lighting and would show half a person's face with bright sunlight falling on it and on the other half he showed deep shadow.

Name of project: *Self portrait (a drawing or painting of yourself)*

Objective: To learn the formula for drawing or painting a face and using that formula to make a self portrait

Getting started

Supplies needed for each participant:

1. oval with neck drawing hand out (see pattern at the end of the lesson)

2. 8" x 11" white paper

3. 4 black 8" x 11" (1 inch wide) strips of construction paper

4. Mirror for each person

5. Lead pencil with eraser

6. Colored pencils

7. Glue

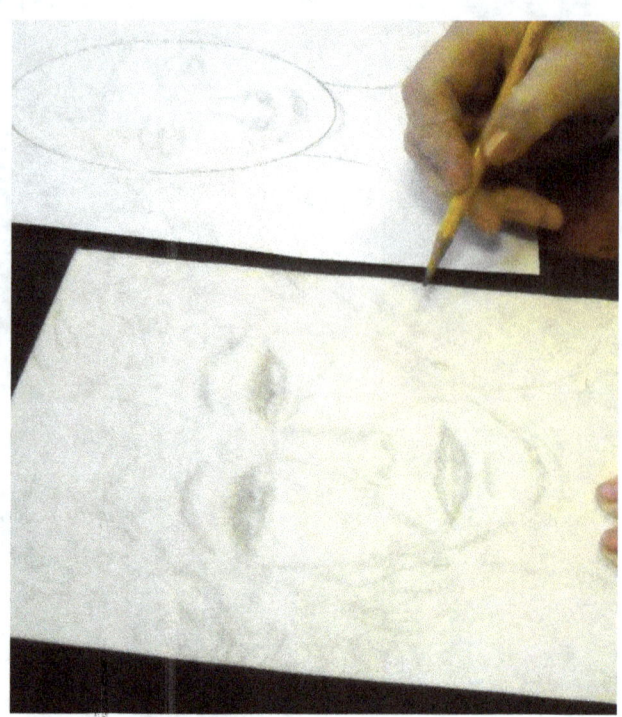

Supplies needed for instructor:

1. Floor easel with sketch pad

2. Black Sharpie marker

3. Masking tape

4. Oval and neck handout taped to sketch pad

5. colored pencils

6. lead drawing pencil

7. CD of instrumental music and CD player (optional)

Before the participants arrive, follow the preparation rules of the art lesson on page 9.

Lesson

1. Introduce the artist and show an example of his work. Emphasize that Rembrandt used a mirror to draw his portrait.

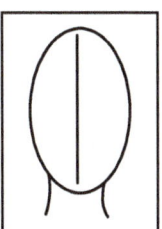

2. Tell the class that almost every artist today and of years ago used a formula for determining the placement of the facial features

3. Using the oval print out and your black marker, show the class how to divide the oval in half vertically.

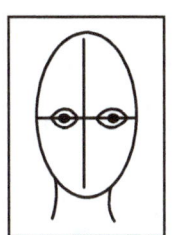

4. Now divide the oval in half horizontally, showing that the eyes are always half way down the face. Put a pupil in the middle of each eye.

5. Draw another line half way from the eye line to the chin.....placement of the end of the nose goes here (each nostril lines up with the tear duct of each eye)

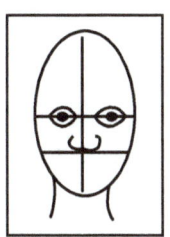

6. Draw another horizontal line half way from the end of the nose to the chin. This is the lip line (the end of the mouth line lines up with the pupil of the eyes) Draw on lips.

7. The ears, on the side of the head, line up with the end of the eye and the end of the nose. Of course, to make your face look like you, you will look in the mirror and add your eyebrows, eyelashes, facial lines, etc.

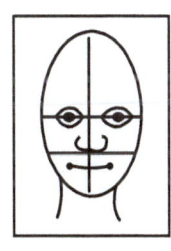

Now, the class is ready to make their own self portrait by following the above formula. The class will use colored pencils to finish their self portrait, trying to match their skin tones, eye color, efftc. At the end, erase the dividing pencil lines.

8. Finish the picture by gluing the four black strips around the border of their self portrait to make a frame.

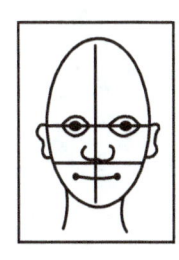

9. This lesson is also good for following up with half of a photo from a magazine given to each artist. They will try to finish the other side of the photo with colored pencils using the formula from the portrait lesson.

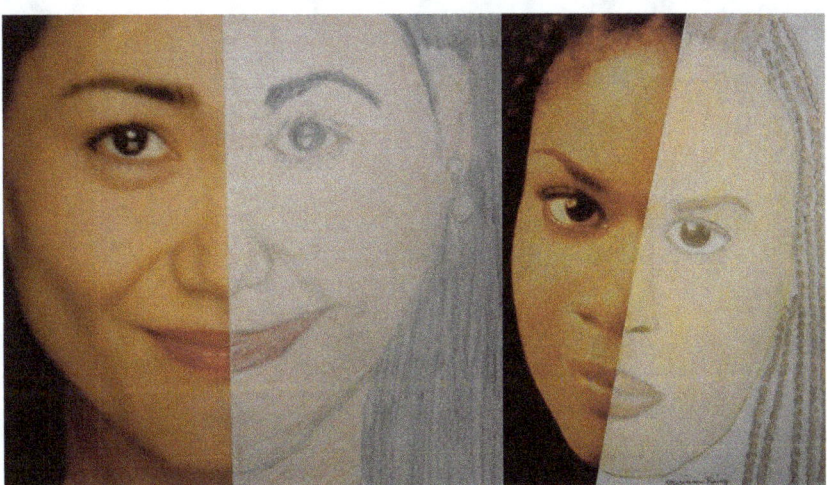

Use with
Rembrandt
lesson

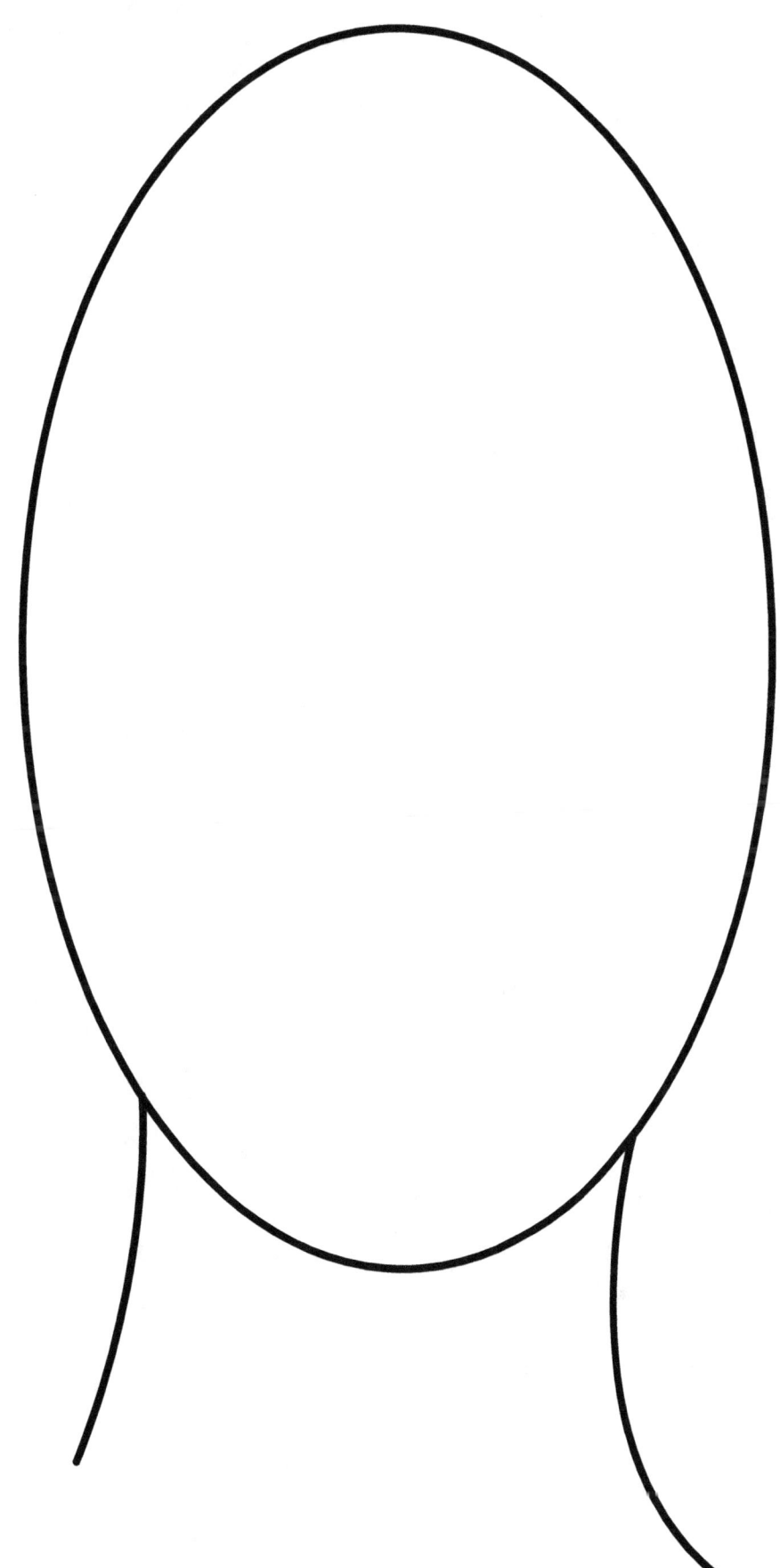

Duplicate page for multiple uses

Bulletin Board Header

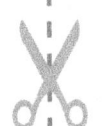

Rembrandt Harmensz van Rijh
1606 – 1669

Rembrandt was famous for painting portraits. He made pictures of himself and everyone in his family. He liked to use strong lighting to add interest to a face, showing half a person's face with bring sunlight falling on it and the other half in a deep shadow.

George Seurat
1859-1891

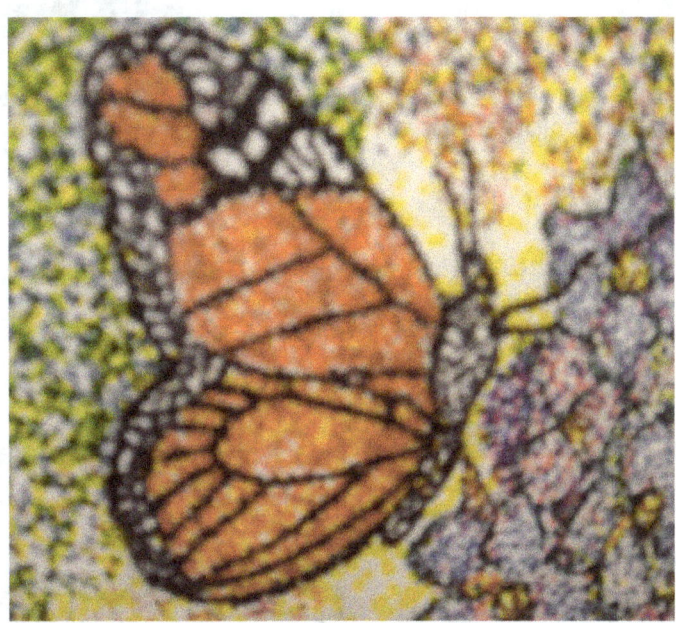

George Seurat was a French Impressionist painter who invented a special style of painting called *pointillism*. Seurat painted pictures using tiny dots of paint color instead of regular brush strokes and solid areas of color. He made different shades of color by painting dots of pure colors close to each other. In this way, he created green by mixing blue and yellow dots. Browns and golds were made with tiny dots of red, blue and orange.

One of Seurat's most famous paintings is titled "<u>Sunday Afternoon on the Island of La Grande Jatte</u>." The painting shows a park with dozens of people walking and relaxing in the grass beneath shady trees. By stepping back from the picture and looking at it from a distance, the thousands of tiny dots seem to blend together to create a shimmering scene. It took the artist nearly two years to complete the seven feet tall by ten foot wide painting.

Name of project: *Pointillism* butterflies

Objectives:
- to create a butterfly using only dots of color
- to instruct students to successfully use markers
- to develop a sense of accomplishment by using the style and technique of George Seurat

Getting started

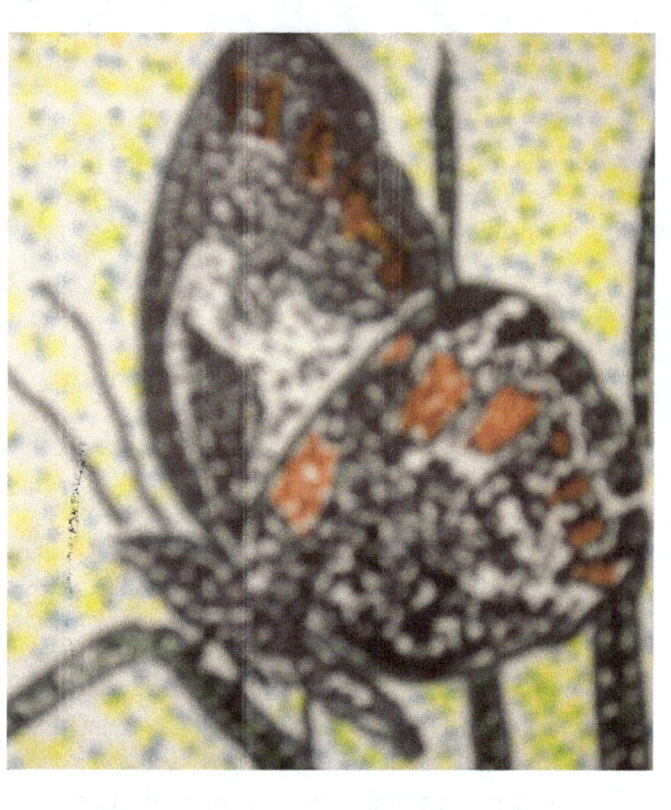

Supplies needed for each participant:

1. 9" x 6" white piece of paper

2. 10" x 5" background colored paper

3. Small tipped colored markers

4. Pencil or black Sharpie marker

5. Butterfly patterns of all kinds (see patterns)

6. Colored pictures of butterflies

Supplies needed for instructor:

1. Floor easel with sketch pad

2. large black marker

3. butterfly patterns

4. 9" x 6" piece of white paper taped to easel pad

5. pictures of butterflies

6. masking tape

7. CD of instrumental music and CD player (optional)

Before the participants arrive, follow the preparation rules of the art lesson on page 9.

Before the participants arrive, follow the preparation rules of the art lesson on page 9.

Never compare your art work to anyone else's—we are all different

George Seurat

Lesson

1. Introduce the artist by reading a short biography and showing examples of his work (e.g. "*Sunday Afternoon on the Island of La Grand Jatte*")

2. Explain the definition of pointillism and show how to use the markers to make dots. Explain and demonstrate that by putting dots close together, areas will look darker, and by placing them farther apart, areas will look lighter.

3. Explain that students will be tracing one or two of the patterns of butterflies onto their white paper. Show them how to do this. Remember, they may also draw butterflies free hand if they wish *(see below A)*.

4. When finished tracing the butterfly pattern, have them fill in the details of the butterfly with the black marker—wing lines, antenna, eyes, etc.(*See below B*).

5. Have each student choose a butterfly picture that is similar to the butterfly pattern that they traced.

6. Have each student pick marker colors that are in the butterfly picture chosen. Remind them that their butterflies should be symmetrical *(see art terminology dictionary)*.

7. Show the class how to start filling in their butterfly with the colored markers using only dots, remembering that the left and right sides will match because they are symmetrical *(see below C)*.

8. When finished, glue each butterfly onto a background color that goes with their butterfly.

9. Have each student show their finished butterfly and sign their name. Display for all to see.

10. Review the terms "*pointillism*" and "*symmetry*" and information about the artist

A

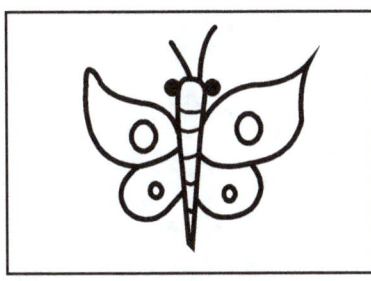

B

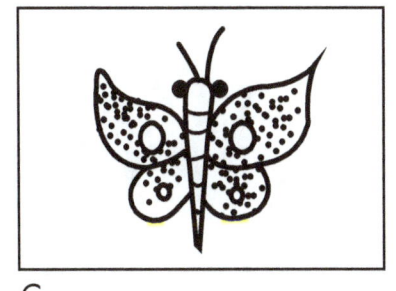

C

George Seurat

77

Use with George Seurat lesson

Bulletin Board Header

Duplicate page for multiple uses

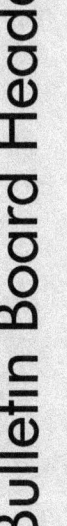

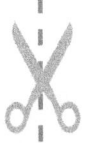

George Seurat 1859-1891

Seurat invented a special style of painting called "pointillism" using only tiny dots of paint and no brush strokes or lines.

Vincent Van Gogh
1853-1890

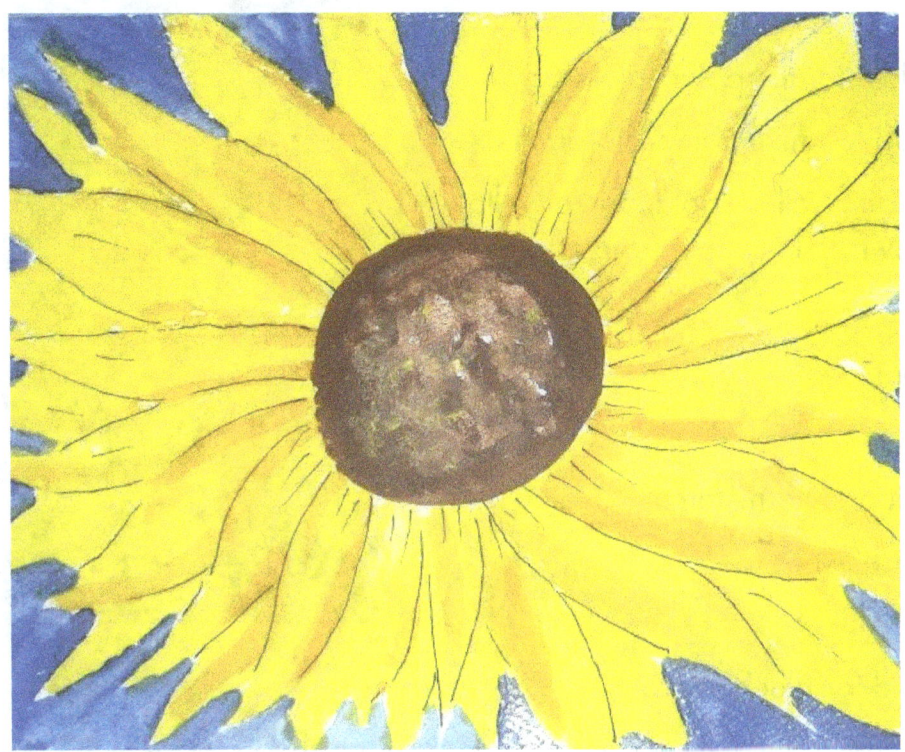

Vincent Van Gogh lived only a short time but he painted nearly 800 paintings in the last ten years of his life. He is well known for his *contrasting* colors and his *"impasto"* style of painting in which he used thick paint. His short quick strokes, which were made with a knife or brush, formed marks with texture. He tried to express his thoughts and emotions in his art work. One of his most famous paintings is entitled "Sunflowers."

Name of project: *Impasto* sunflowers

Objectives:
- To create a sunflower painting using the *"impasto"* method of painting
- To give students the opportunity to experience Van Gogh's style of painting.

Getting started

Supplies needed for each participant:

1. 4" x 6" (or larger) piece of water color paper

2. Paper plate for the paint colors

3. Paper cup for mixing impasto paint

4. Acrylic paint: yellow, gold/darker yellow, blue, brown, and copper/darker brown

5. Paper towel

6. Water pan

7. Art smock

8. Tablespoon of corn starch

9. Paint brush(es)

10. Popsicle stick

11. Pencil and/or black Sharpie

12. Brown, blue or yellow background paper for finished picture

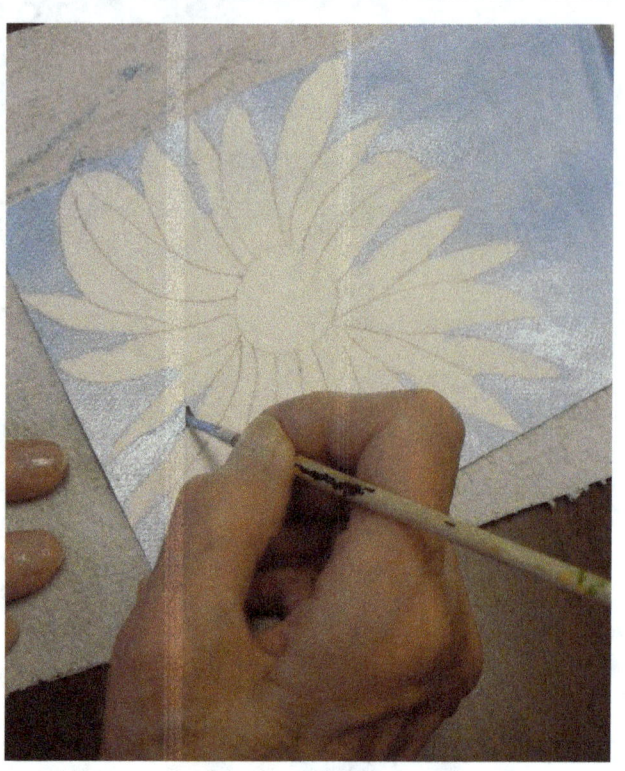

Supplies needed for instructor:

1. Floor easel with sketch pad

2. Large black marker

3. Box of corn starch

4. 4" x 6" piece of *water color* paper

5. Paint brush(es) and popsicle stick

6. Paper cup for mixing

7. Yellow, gold, blue and shades of brown acrylic paint

8. Glue

9. Pan of water

10. Art smock

11. Masking tape for securing papers of students who need it

12. Several pictures of different sunflowers and an artificial one

13. CD of instrumental music and CD player (optional)

Before the participants arrive, follow the preparation rules of the art lesson on page 9.

Lesson

1. Introduce the artist with a brief biography and show an example of his work

2. Show the artificial sunflower, pointing out the shape of the petals

3. Explain impasto paint and show how to mix it (add a small amount of water to cornstarch and mix with popsicle stick)

4. Squeeze out a dab of every acrylic paint color onto the students' plates

5. Instruct the students to draw a circle the size of a half dollar with a pencil or the sharpie marker at or near the middle of the page *(see image A below)*.

6. Next they should add petal shapes all the way around the circle. Make sure the petals are at least two inches long *(see image B below)*. Continue adding petals until the shape of a sunflower is finished. Some of the petals should go off the edge of the page. Students may also add a second flower *(see image C below)*.

7. Using the blue paint, students should fill in the "sky" background behind their finished sunflower drawing.

8. Show the class how to use the popsicle stick to fill in each petal using the yellow paint and cornstarch mixture to make the impasto texture.

9. When finished, have them use the gold acrylic paint to outline the sunflower petals with the paint brush to emphasize the petal edges *(see image D below)*. The brown and copper paint can then be used to dot the center of the sunflower with the paintbrush to represent seeds.

10. When dry, mount the finished sunflower onto the colored back ground paper.

11. Make sure each student has their name on their painting.

12. Arrange on a bulletin board for all to see.

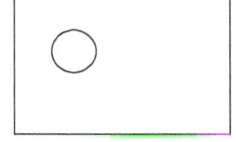 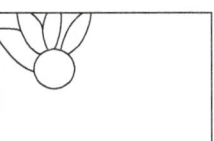 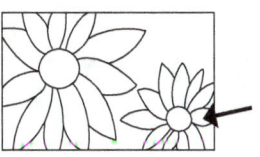 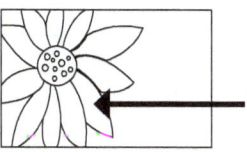

A B C D

Bulletin Board Header

Duplicate page for multiple uses

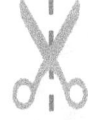

Vincent Van Gogh   1853-1890

Van Gogh is one of the most famous painters of all time.

Even though he lived a short life, he painted approximately 800 paintings. He is known for his short, quick strokes using thick paint and a knife or brush.

Andy Warhol
1930-1966

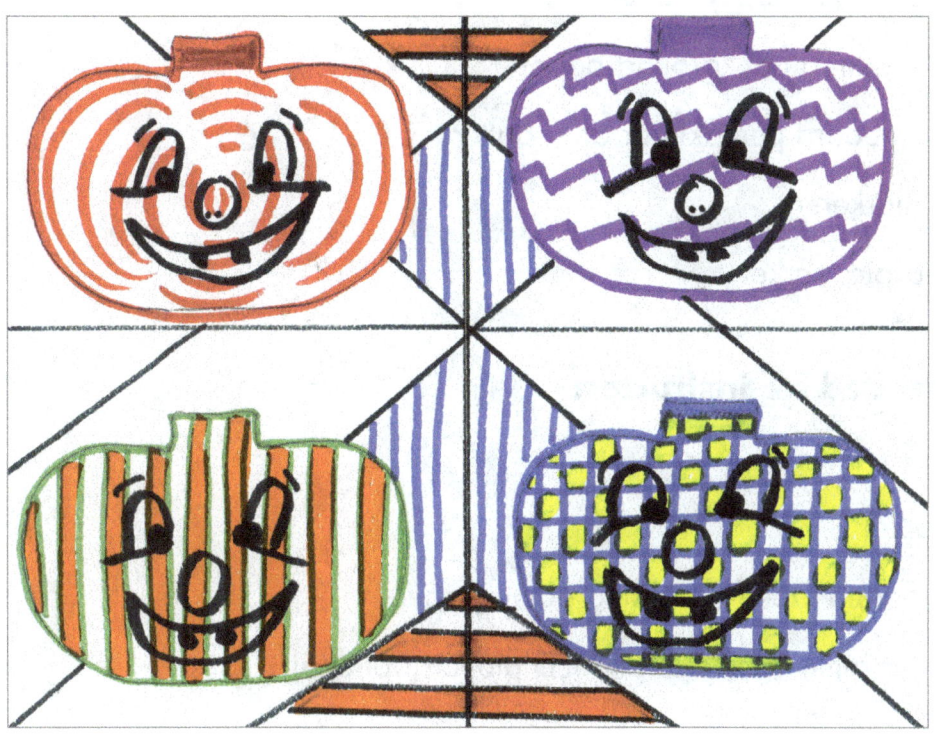

The American artist Andy Warhol was famous for paintings of celebrities and famous people. Warhol's paintings often start with photographs of a famous person. Many of his paintings show repeats of the same image colored in different ways. His most famous works are pictures of Marilyn Monroe and a red and white Campbell's soup can.

Name of project: *Four shapes Andy Warhol style*

Objectives: to create a repeating image by tracing a pattern four times and designing it in four different ways.

Getting started

Supplies needed for each participant:

1. 11" x 8.5" white heavy paper

2. 12" x 9" colored background paper

3. 3" x 4" tagboard pumpkin or any pattern

4. Colored markers

5. Black Sharpie marker

Supplies needed for instructor:

1. Floor easel with sketch pad

2. Black marker

3. Roll of masking tape for holding down paper.

4. A CD of instrumental music and CD player (optional).

Before the participants arrive, follow the preparation rules of the art lesson on page 9.

Just do your best!

Lesson

1. Introduce the artist and show an example of his work, emphasizing and pointing out the repeating of the same image, but with different colors (e.g. Marilyn Monroe).

2. Have the participants trace their tagboard pattern four times with the black marker onto their white sheet of paper.

3. Explain to the class that they will design their pattern with the colored markers in four different ways using any kinds of line (zigzag, curvy, etc.), or designs such as flowers, shapes.

4. Have each participant write their name at the bottom of the page.

5. The instructor will glue each participant's finished picture onto the colored background sheet.

6. Have each person show their finished picture.

7. Review the name of the artist and emphasize and compliment the different designs of each participant.

8. Praise the class for making a picture like the style of Andy Warhol.

9. Display the finished art work and a brief paragraph about the artist Andy Warhol on a bulletin board where everyone can see it.

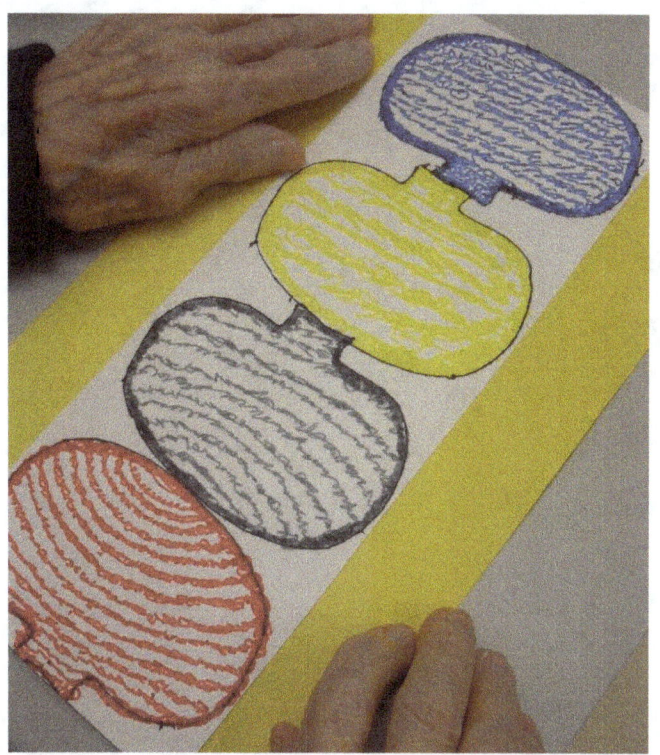

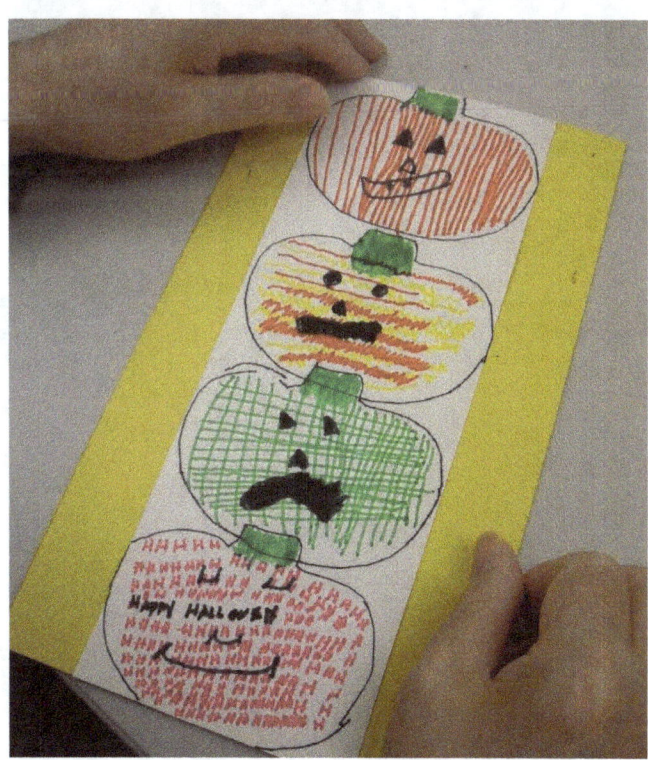

Resources: Project Patterns

Use with Andy Warhol lesson

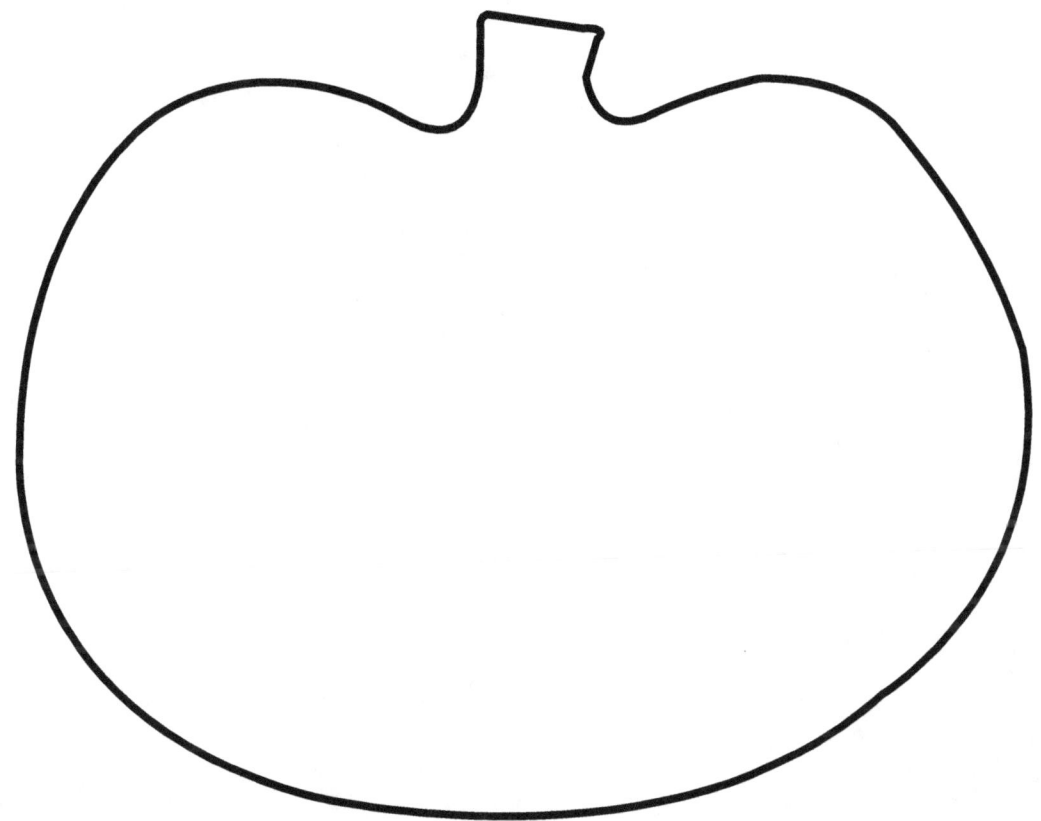

Bulletin Board Header

Duplicate page for multiple uses

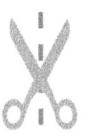

Andy Warhol 1930-1987

Warhol loved making paintings showing repeats of the same image colored in different ways.

Clay Pinch Pot

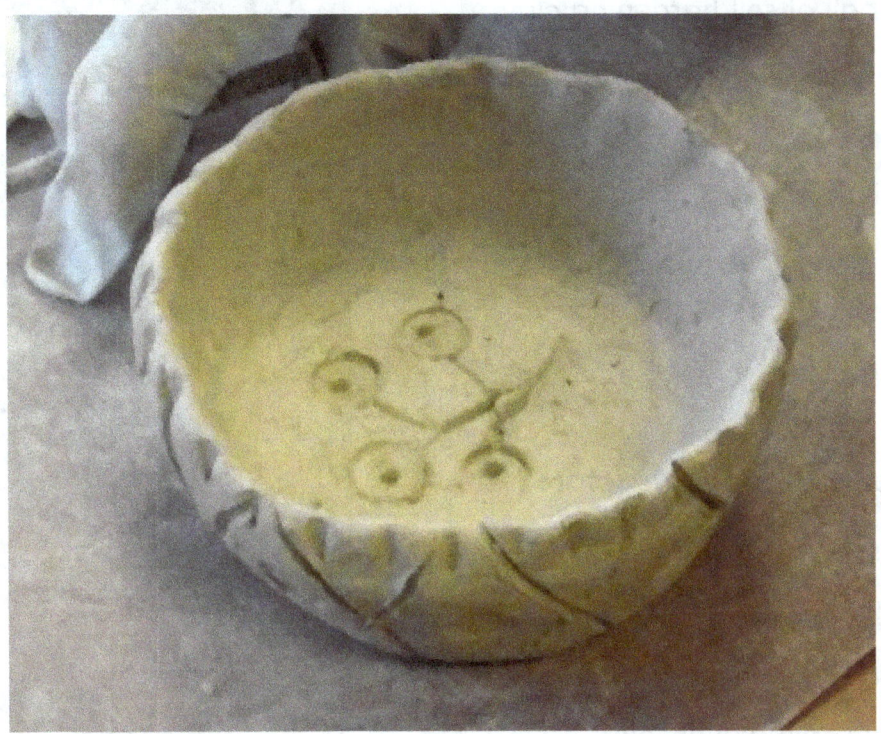

The potter's wheel has only existed for about 4000 years. Before that, pinching and coiling of clay were some of the main methods for constructing clay objects and containers. Pinch pots are one of the most direct methods for people to interact with clay. By pushing and pinching, people learn to rely on their fingers to mold the clay into some form of art object. By creating pinch pots, we are able to use our senses of touch *and* sight. We learn to rely on our fingers to give us a feeling for the clay.

Name of project: *Pinch pot*

Objective: to create a pinch pot by using our fingers and the senses of touch and sight.

Getting started

Supplies needed for each participant:

1. 2 – 2.5" ball of self hardening clay

2. Piece of vinyl or canvas to set under the clay

3. Small water pan

4. Tools for making texture: nail, toothpick, popsickle stick, disposable gloves, etc.

5. Art smock

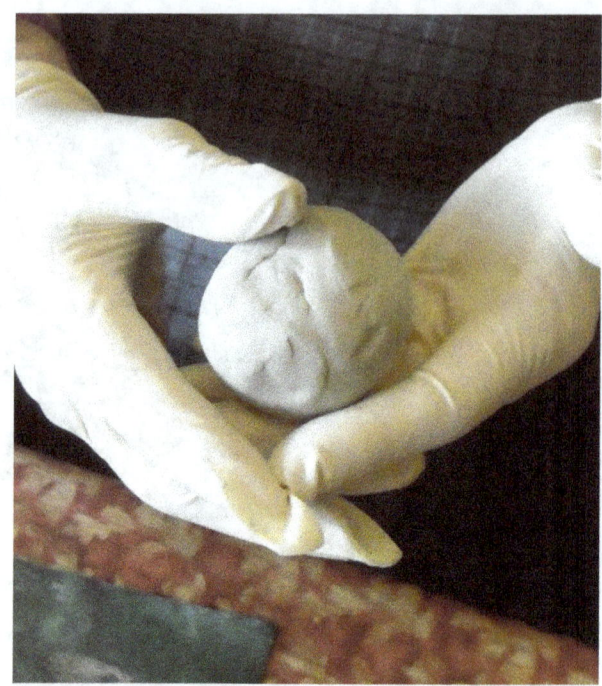

Supplies needed for instructor:

1. Example(s) of a pinch pot

2. Ball of self hardening clay

3. Clay tools...nail, toothpick, pop sickle stick, disposable gloves, etc.

4. Small pan of water

5. Vinyl or canvas mat (6" x 6" piece to put clay on)

6. Art smock

7. Easel with sketch pad

8. Large black marker

9. CD of instrumental music and a CD player (optional)

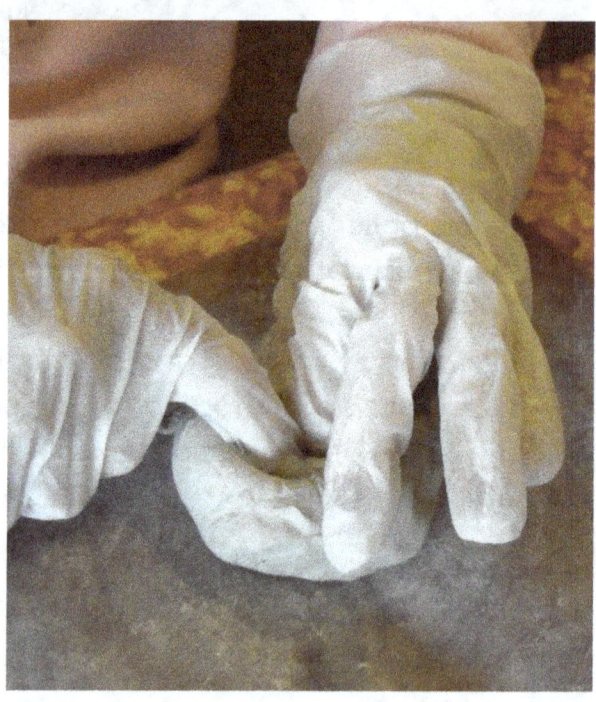

Before the participants arrive, follow the preparation rules of the art lesson on page 9.

Lesson

1. Give a brief description and history of pinch pots.

2. Show some examples of pinch pots.

3. Put on your gloves and show the class how to insert their thumb into the middle of the clay ball by pushing down as hard as they can, making sure to leave a one fourth thickness at the bottom. Some students may need help with this part.

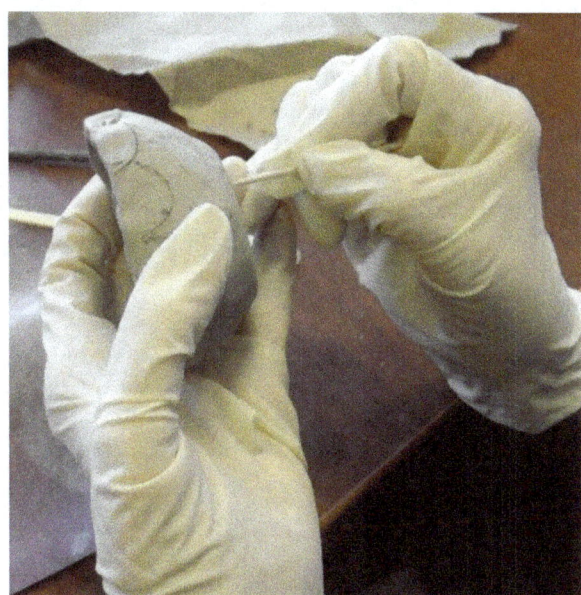

4. With your fingers, begin pinching (thumb on the inside of the bowl and fingers close together on the outside). Begin pinching the clay, turning the piece as you pinch. This will help you keep an even thickness in the walls of the piece.

5. Continue this process until you have the desired shape.

6. When finished, have the class gently tap the bottom of their pot on their vinyl mat to flatten the bottom of their pot.

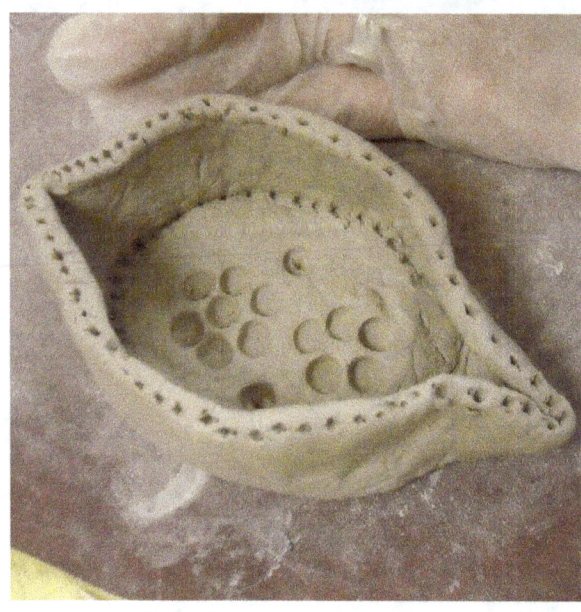

7. Show the class how to use their tools. Each tool makes a different texture (see reference photos at right).

8. When the class is finished, have them put their names on the bottoms of their pinch pots with the tooth picks.

9. Place the finished pinch pots on a shelf to dry.

10. The pinch pots can be painted with acrylic paints when they are dry.

Clay Pinch Pot

A pinch pot is formed by "pinching" your fingers forming the walls of the clay pot and then turning the piece as you pinch. Pinch pots are some of the oldest archaeological artifacts found. Many civilizations used pinch pots for functional use and some still do today.

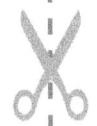

Mosaic

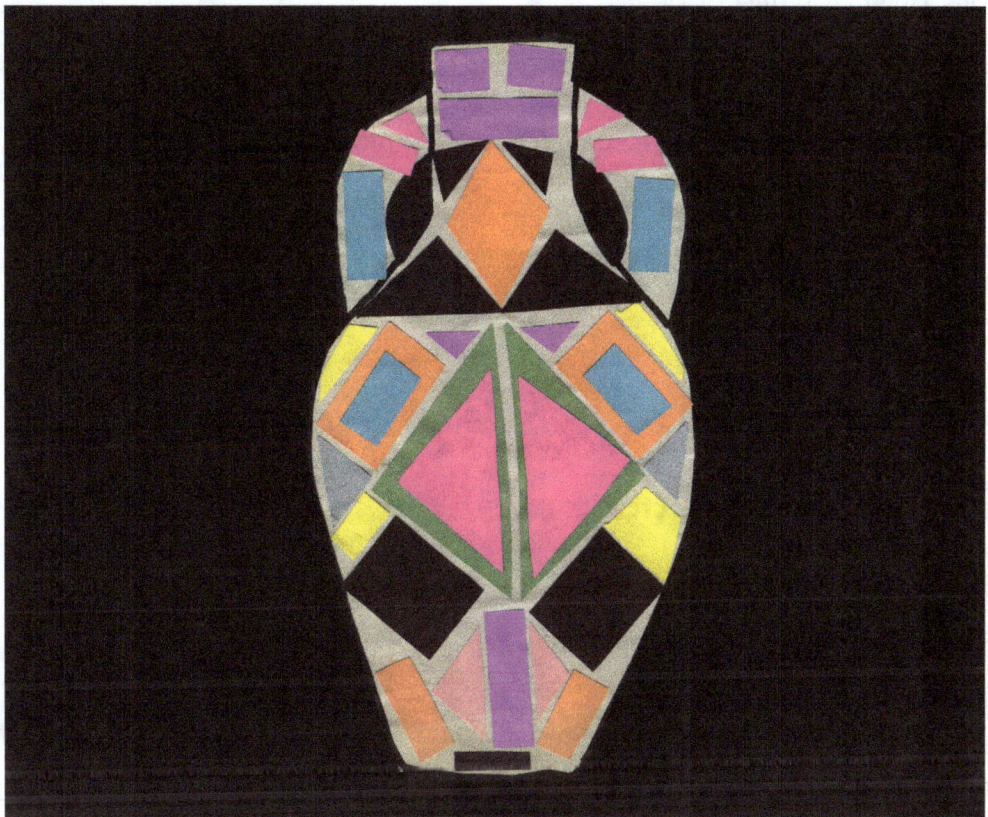

Mosaic is a type of surface decoration used on walls, tables, and walkways where little bits of colored stone or glass are pressed into cement to make a design or pattern. Paper, beans, seeds, egg shells, or other materials may be also be used.

Name of project: Mosaic vase

Objectives: To create a design or pattern on a vase shape. (Note: this project is for those who can cut and glue. Choose participants who do not frustrate easily)

Getting started

Supplies needed for each participant:

1. 8" x 10" gray or white paper

2. 9" x 12" black paper

3. Several colors of one inch strip colored paper (flourescent works very well)

4. Pair of scissors

5. Small bottle of Elmer's glue

6. Black Sharpie pen

7. A vase shape pattern

Supplies needed for instructor:

1. Example of mosaic(s)..dish, picture, etc.

2. 4 or 5 vase patterns made of sturdy cardboard

3. Large black marker

4. Another full set of the same materials as the participants

5. CD of instrumental music and a CD player (optional)

Before the participants arrive, follow the preparation rules of the art lesson on page 9.

Art smart

Lesson

1. Write the word "Mosaic" on the easel sketch pad with the large black marker and explain the meaning.

2. Show examples of mosaic.

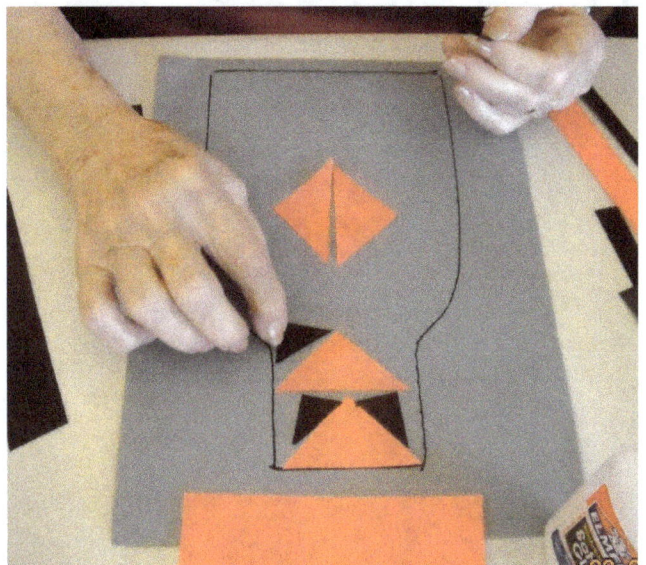

4. Demonstrate how to trace one of the vase patterns on to the grey or white paper with the black sharpie.

5. Demonstrate how to cut off square, triangle or rectangle pieces of paper from their colored strips of paper (see example below)

6. Instruct the class to begin making mosaic designs or patterns on their vases using pieces of colored paper. There should be spaces between each glued piece to represent grout.

   Note: when gluing, put a drop of glue on the gray paper instead of the colored piece. It is much easier than trying to put glue on the back of each cut piece.

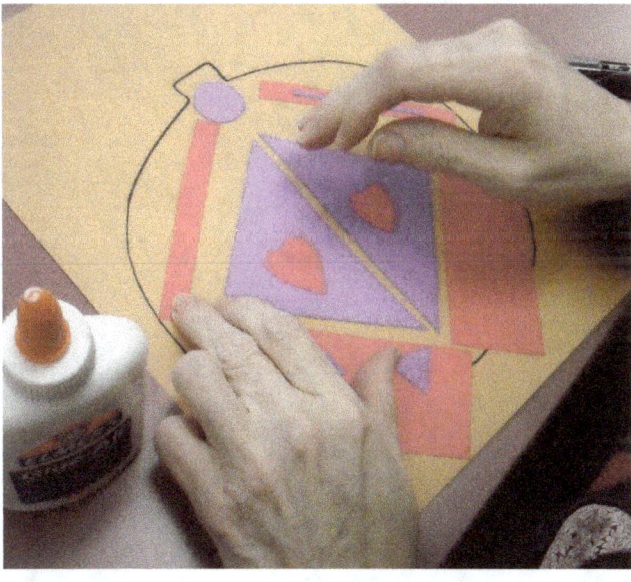

7. When finished with their mosaic designs, have the students cut out the vase shapes and glue them to the 8" x 11" papers.

8. Have them sign their names and show their finished mosaics to the class. Be sure to emphasize the differences in each one.

9. Display for all to see.

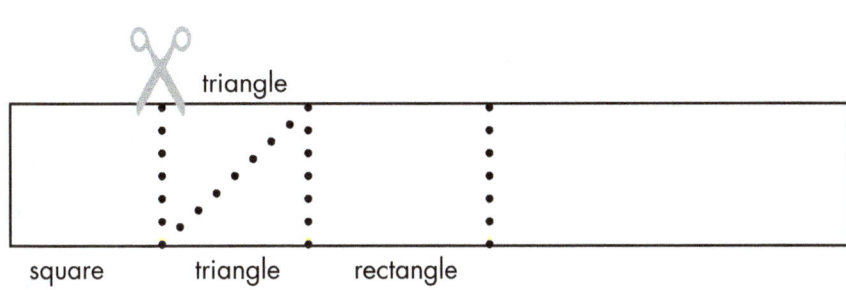

Use with
Mosaic lesson

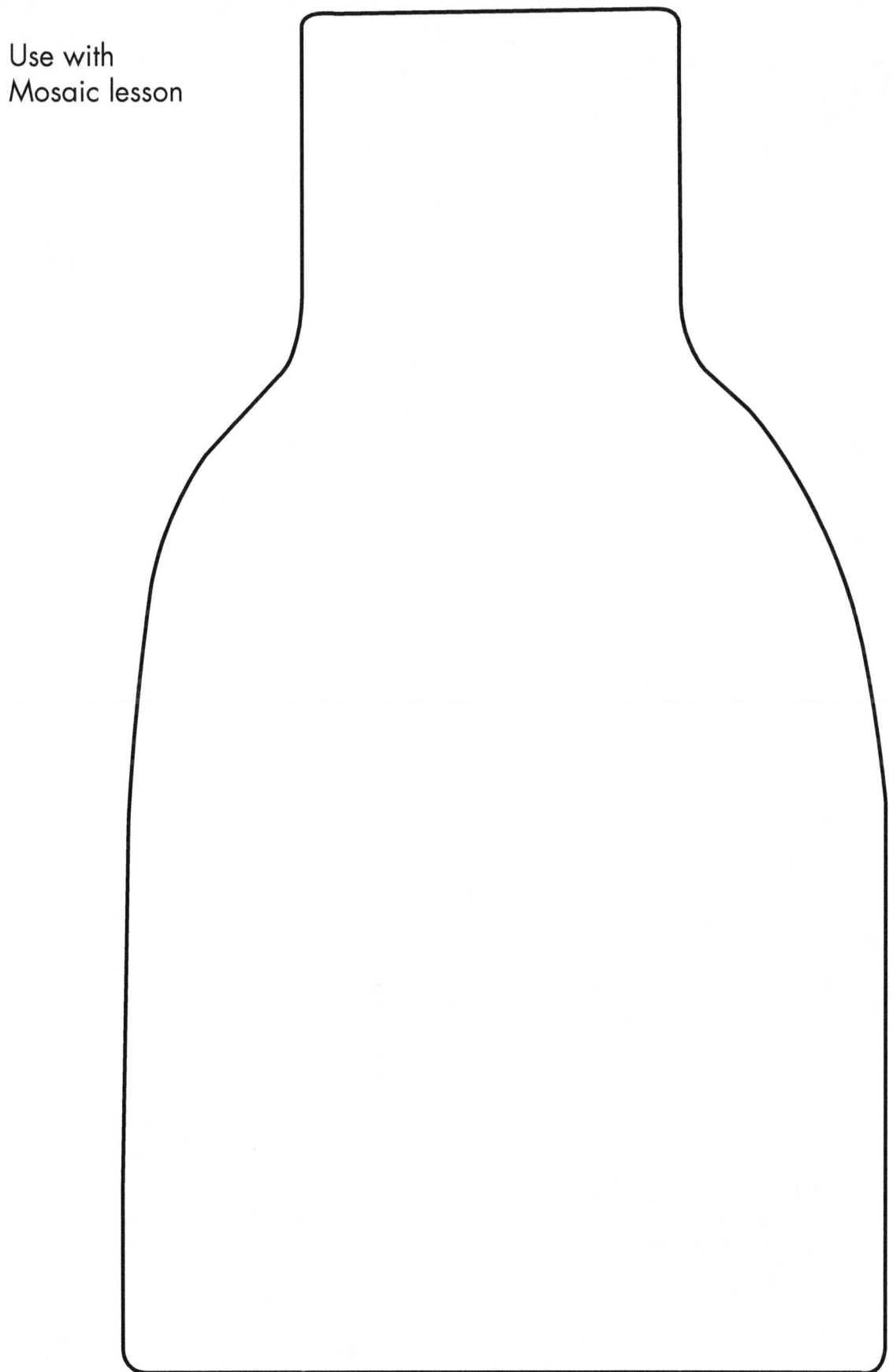

Duplicate page for multiple uses

Use with
Mosaic lesson

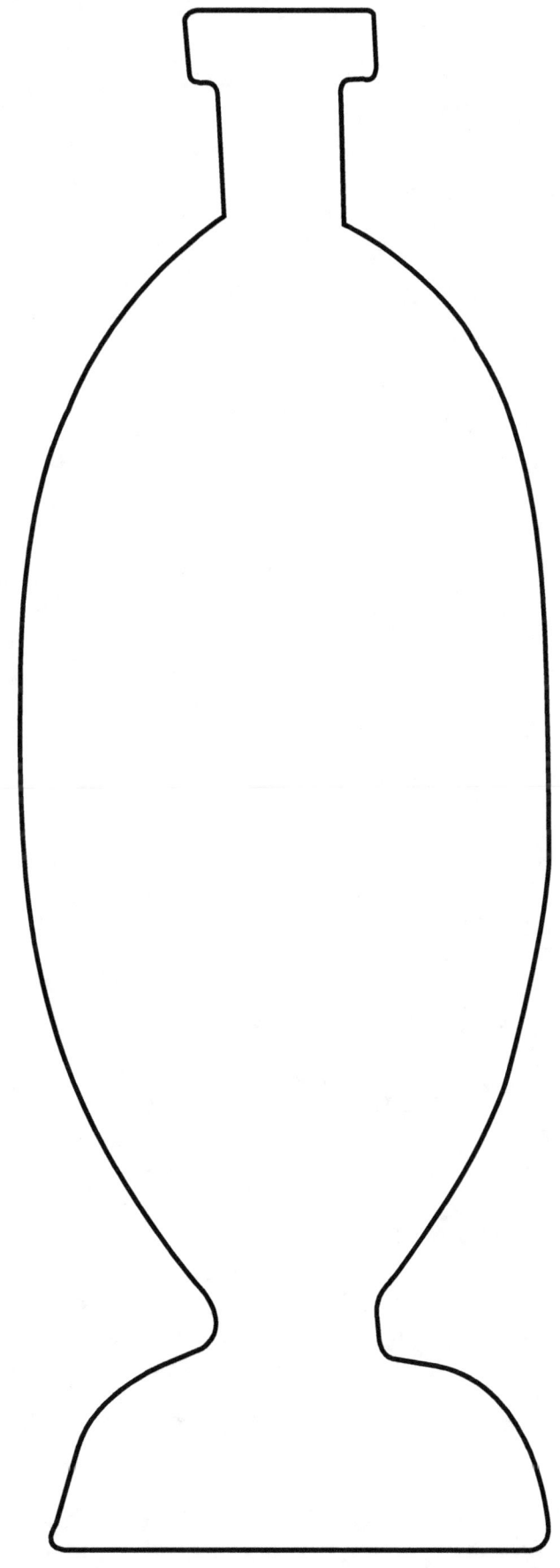

Use with
Mosaic lesson

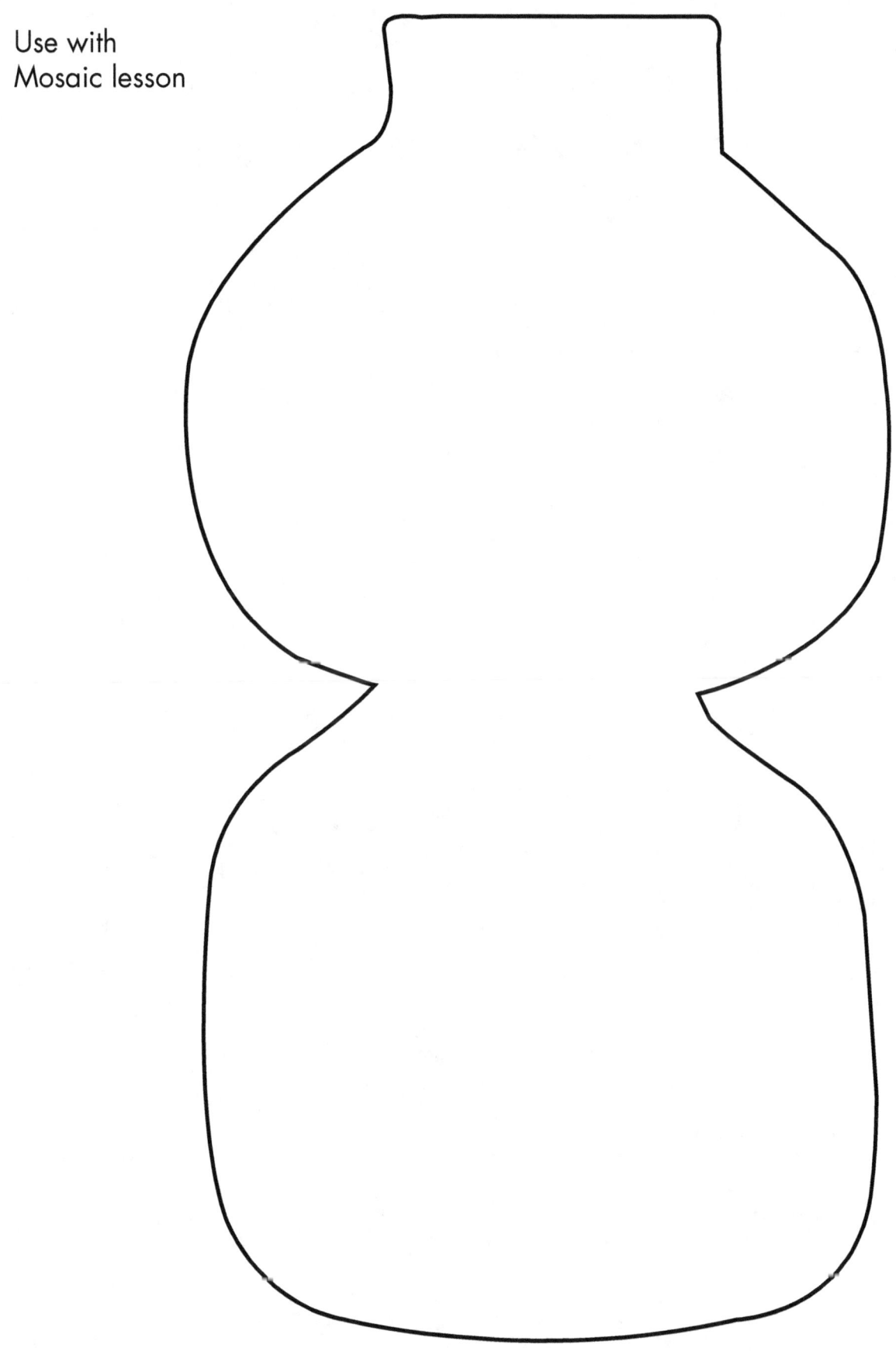

Use with
Mosaic lesson

Bulletin Board Header

Duplicate page for multiple uses

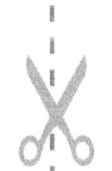

Mosaic

Mosaic is the art of creating images with small pieces of colored glass, stone, paper, or other material. It may be a technique of decorative art, interior design or spiritual significance as in a cathedral.

Primary and Secondary Colors

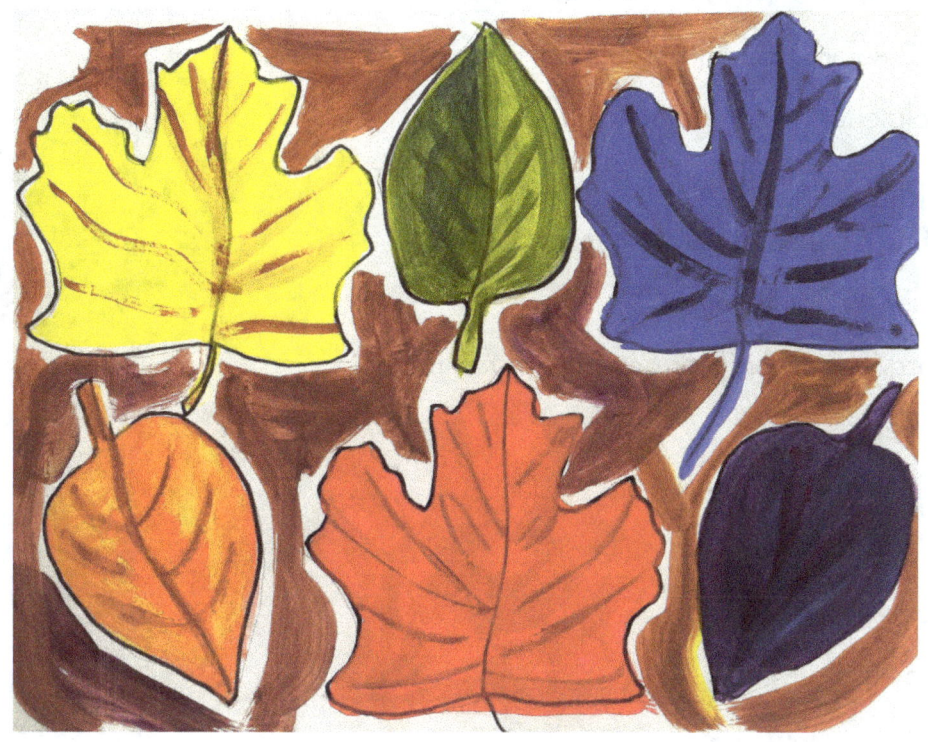

Primary colors (red, yellow, and blue) are the basic colors from which all other colors are made. By mixing two of the primary colors together, the *secondary colors* (orange, green and purple) are made.

Name of project: *Mixing colors*

Objectives: to create the secondary colors orange, green and purple by mixing combinations of the three primary colors, red, yellow and blue together.

Getting started

Supplies needed for each participant:

1. 6" x 10" sheet of white construction paper

2. 8" x 11" colored background paper

3. Paper plate for mixing paint

4. Paint brush (#7 or similar)

5. Blob of red, blue and yellow tempera paint

6. Container for holding water

7. Tagboard leaf pattern(s)or any pattern for tracing

8. Black Sharpie marker

9. 8" x 11" colored paper for background

10. Pair of scissors

11. Art smock or apron

12. Paper towel(s)

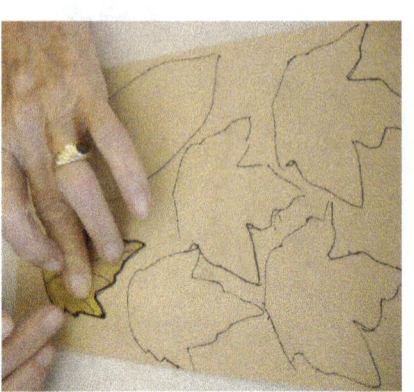

Supplies needed for instructor:

1. A visual example of the primary and secondary colors (jars of red, blue and yellow paint)

2. Leaf pattern (different shapes and kinds)

3. Scissors

4. Paper plate

5. Paint brush (#7 or similar)

6. Roll of masking tape for holding down papers

7. Floor easel with sketch pad

8. Black marker

9. Bottle of glue

10. Paper towels

11. Definition of primary and secondary colors for display board

12. A CD of instrumental music and CD player *(optional)*

Before the participants arrive, follow the preparation rules of the art lesson on page 9.

Lesson

1. Give the definition of the primary (the first colors red, blue and yellow) from which all other colors are made and secondary (orange, green and purple – a mixture of two primary colors) and write the words primary and secondary colors on the sketch pad.

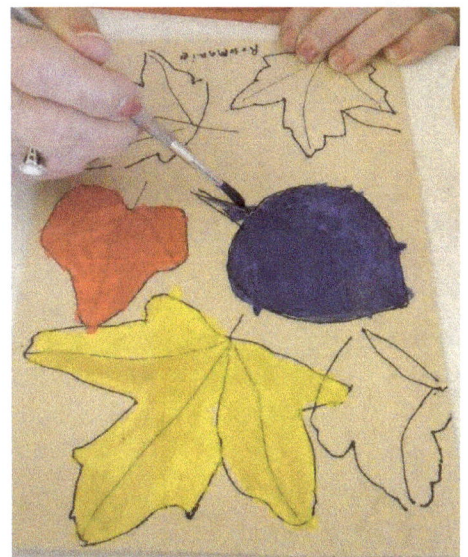

2. Explain that the participants are going to make the three secondary colors today using different mixtures of the primary colors.

3. The instructor will trace a leaf pattern 6 times onto the sketch pad with the black marker.

4. The students will then trace their leaf pattern onto their white sheet of paper 6 times with the black marker.

5. Select three of the of the traced leaf patterns and paint one red, then blue, then yellow. Give students time to do the same.

6. Demonstrate how to mix one part red to one part yellow with the paint brush to make the secondary color orange, and then paint one of the leaves orange. Always add the darker color to the lighter one. Rinse out your brush while the students mix their own orange paint.

7. Demonstrate how to mix one part yellow to one part blue to make the secondary color green, and then paint one of the leaves green. Rinse out the brush while students mix their own green paint.

8. Demonstrate how to mix one part blue to one part red to make the secondary color purple, and then will paint one of the leaves purple. Rinse out your brush while the students mix their own purple paint. Cut out the 6 leaves when dry.

9. Glue the corners of each painted leaf onto a colored background paper.

10. Emphasize that we have now made three secondary colors by mixing different combinations of primary colors together.

11. Have students sign their names on their paper and hold up their finished pictures.

12. Praise the class for their wonderful accomplishment and great listening skills!

13. Display the primary and secondary colored leaves with the definition of primary and secondary colors.

Use with
Primary and
Secondary
Colors lesson

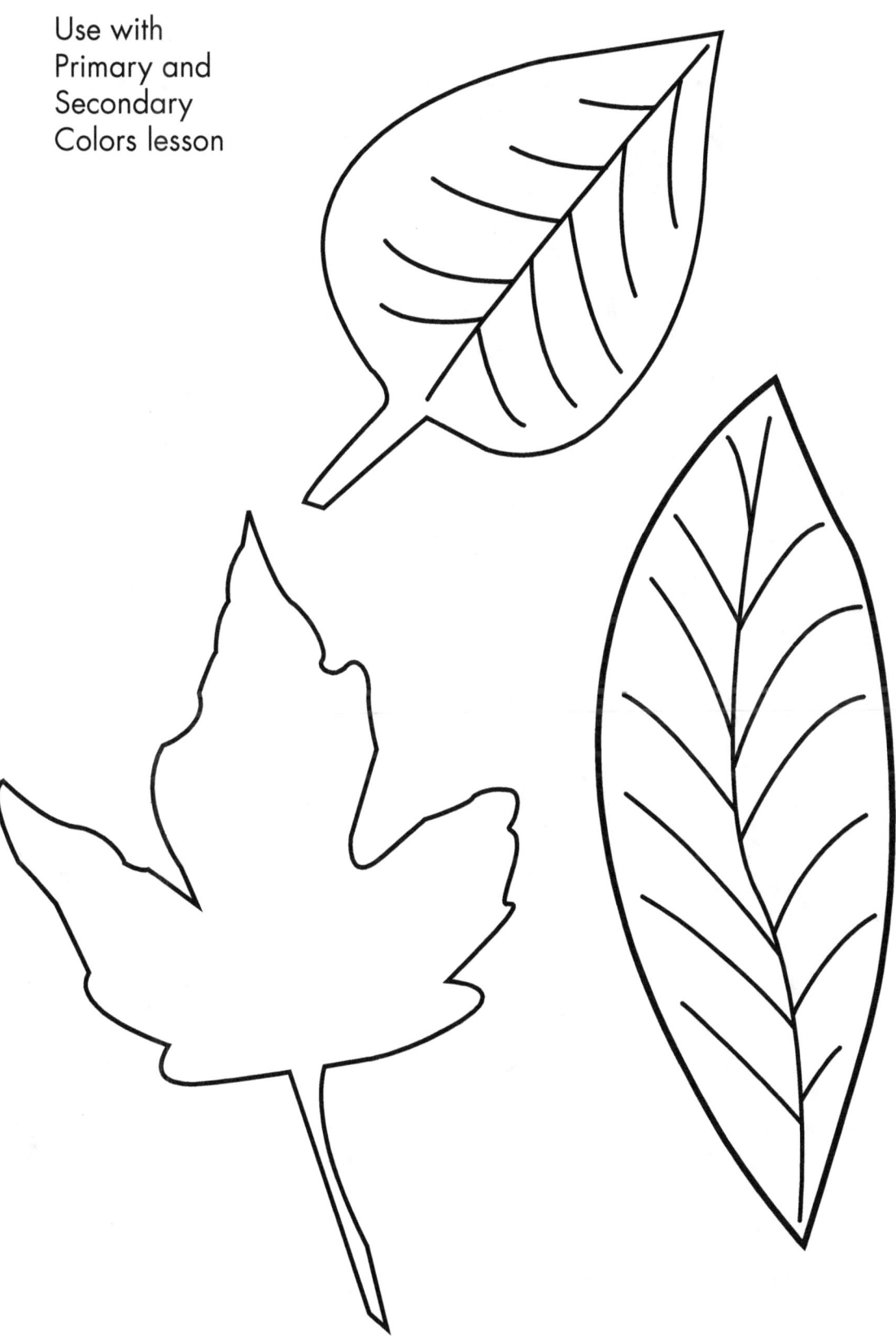

Bulletin Board Header

Duplicate page for multiple uses

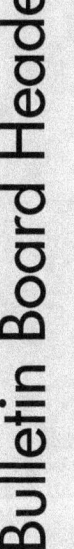

Primary and Secondary Colors

The primary colors (red, blue and yellow) are the basic colors from which all other colors are made. Mixed in varying ways, these make other colors like green, orange and purple.

Scratch Board Art

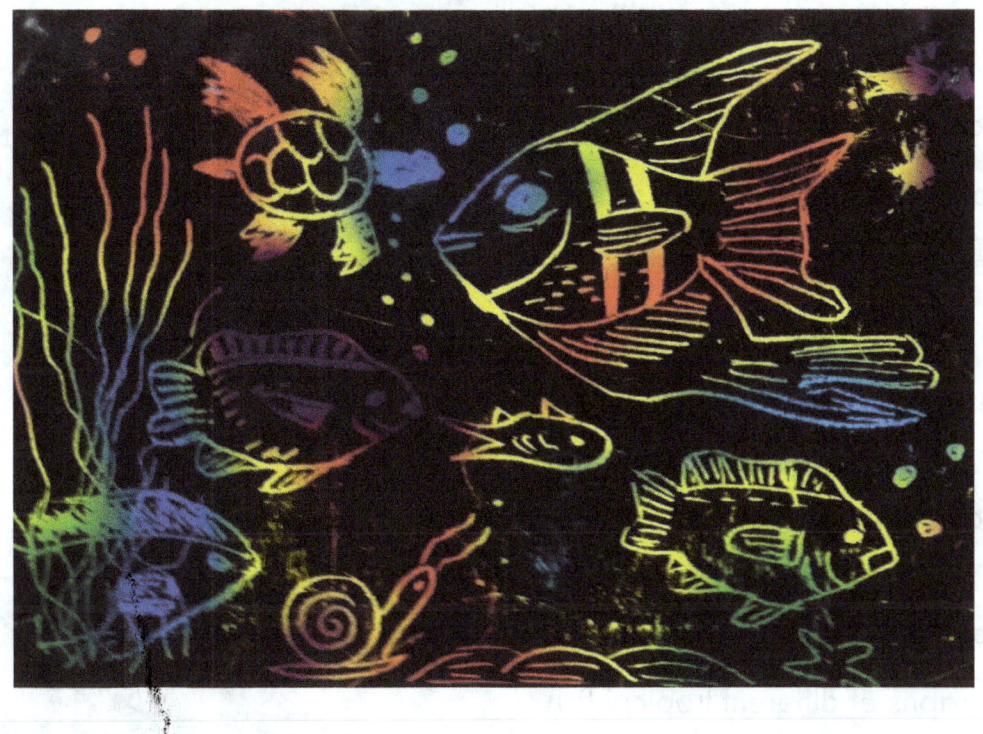

Scratch boards are boards of various thickness coated with a fine white clay or rainbow ink colors and then covered with an opaque black ink. Dramatic drawings can be created by scratching texture and lines through the black ink with a small pointed wooden or metal stick.

Name of project: *Scratch board fish*

Objective: to create a fish aquarium picture using the scratch method

Getting started

Supplies needed for each participant:

1. One piece of 5" x 7" scratch paper

2. Pointed wooden stick

3. Fish tracers

4. Pictures of different tropical fish

5. Kleenex

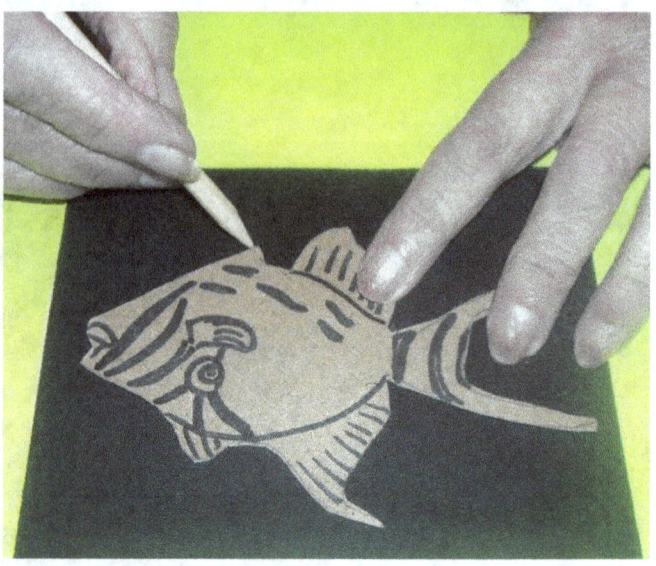

Supplies needed for instructor:

1. A brief explanation of a scratch board

2. An example of a finished scratched fish

3. Several fish patterns for tracing

4. Photographs of different tropical fish

5. One piece, 5" x 7" scratch paper

6. Wooden pointed stick

7. Bottle of glue

8. Kleenex

9. Colored background papers

10. Floor easel with sketch pad

11. Large black marker

12. Roll of masking tape

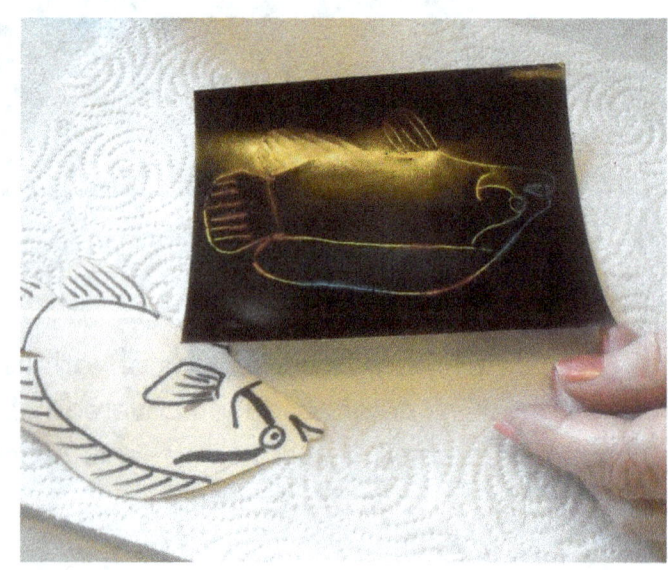

13. A CD of instrumental music and a CD player (optional)

Before the participants arrive, follow the preparation rules of the art lesson on page 9.

Lesson

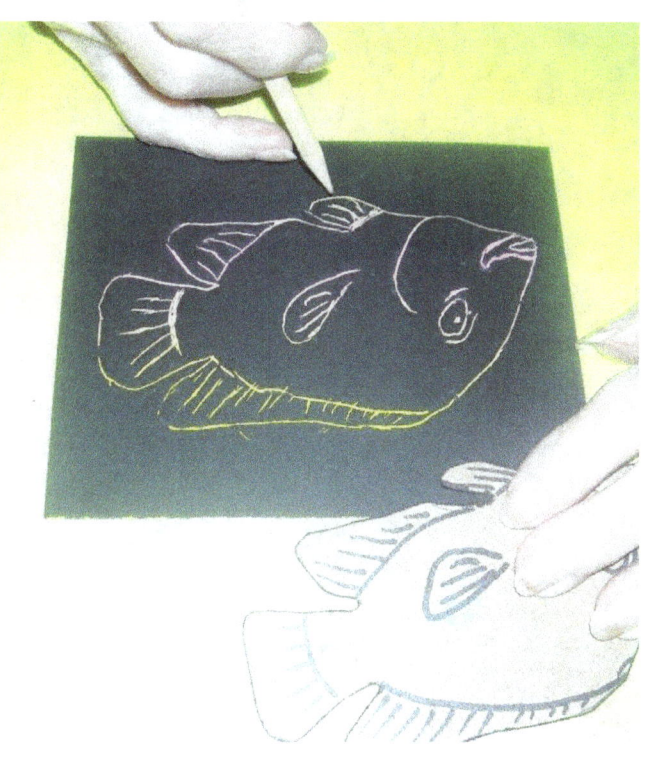

1. Give a brief explanation of a scratch board

2. Explain why it is important to hold your picture down with the fingers of the opposite hand on the kleenex to avoid getting oil from your fingers on the paper because the oil will make it very difficult to scratch the surface(show them this with your own hand)

3. Talk about an aquarium and what is in one

4. Tape a piece of black scratch paper to your easel pad

5. Trace around one of the fish patterns with the wooden stick *(See picture on page 126)*

6. Tell the class to notice the color that shows after scratching the line. *(See picture on page 126)*

7. Explain that there are many colors hiding beneath the surface of the paper and by scratching with the stick they will appear. *(See picture above)*

8. Instruct the class to choose fish pattern(s) of different sizes

9. Instruct the class to begin tracing around their fish patterns with the stick onto their scratch board.

10. By looking at the photographs of the fish scattered on the tables the class can see what designs to scratch on their fish.

11. Instruct the class to include other things in their picture that they may find in an aquarium (seaweed, shells, marbles, stones, etc.)

12. Finish by gluing each finished scratch art onto colored background paper and scratching their name onto the paper.

13. Display for all to see.

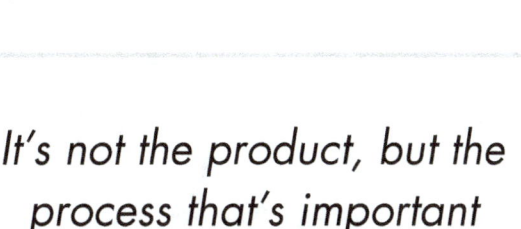

It's not the product, but the process that's important

Use with
Scratch Board
lesson

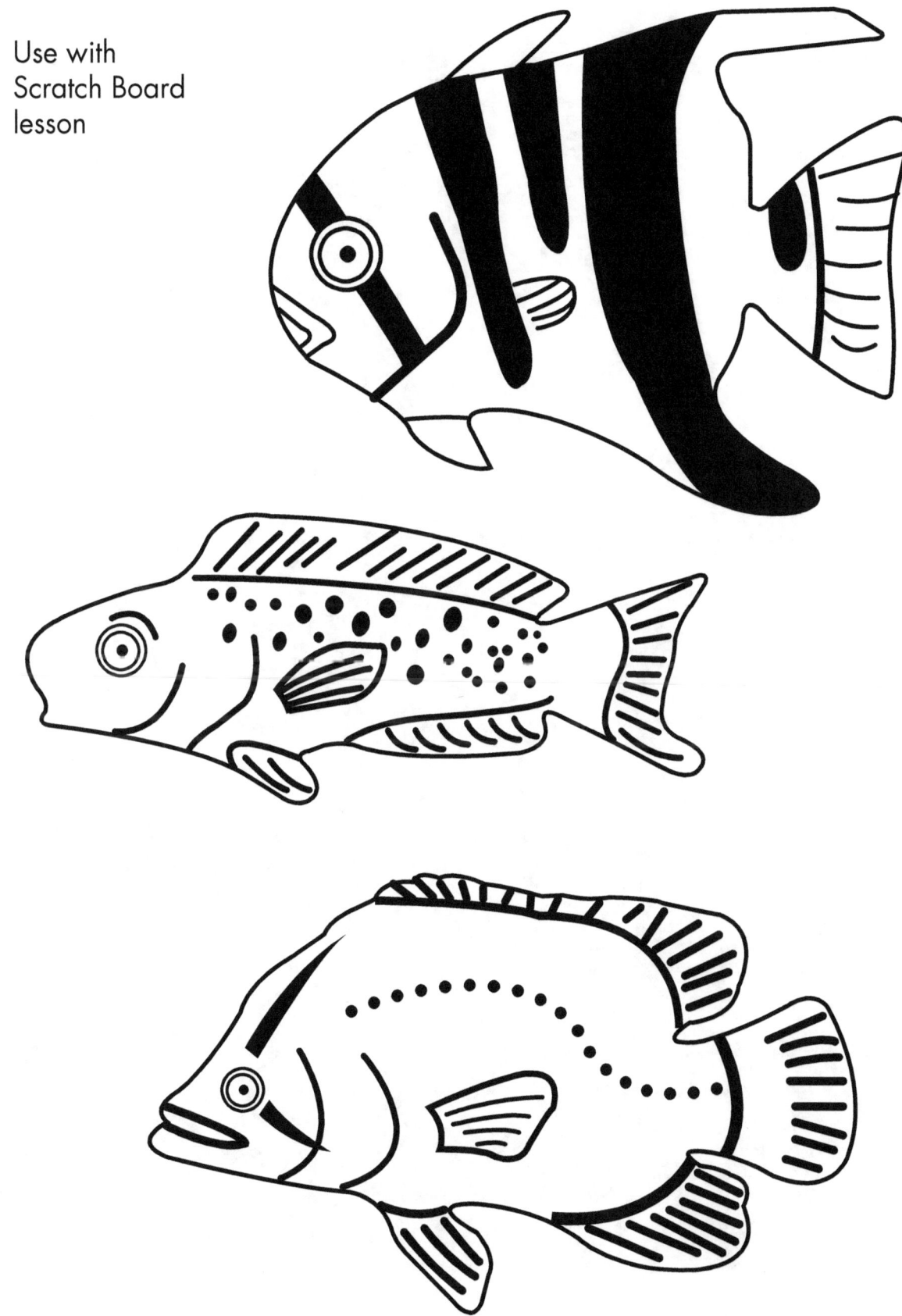

Bulletin Board Header

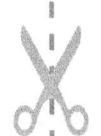

Scratch Boards

Scratch boards are boards of various thickness coated with a fine white clay or rainbow ink colors and then covered with an opaque black ink. Dramatic drawings can be created by scratching texture and/ or lines through the black ink with a small pointed wooden or metal stick.

Stenciling a Tulip

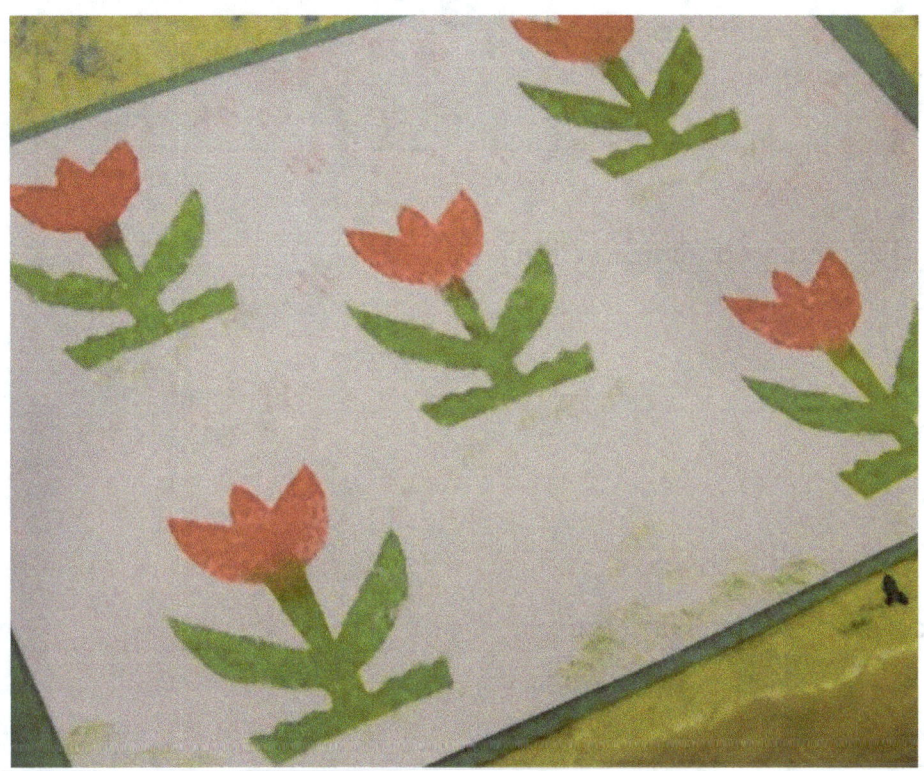

Stenciling is the art of cutting out a design or picture from a sheet of heavier material such as tagboard, plastic, or metal, and then transferring that picture or pattern to another surface such as paper, material, or glass by using a stencil brush and paint.

Name of project: *Stenciling a tulip*

Objectives:

•To create an original tulip stencil and transfer the stencil image to another surface by using a stencil brush and paint.

• To develop confidence and creativity.

• To encourage individuality.

Getting started

Supplies needed for each participant:

1. 9" x 11" heavy white construction or water color paper.

2. 4" x 6" piece of tag board folded in half

3. 10" x 12" colored construction paper for background

4. Scissors

5. Black sharpie

6. Paper plate

7. One or two stencil brushes

8. Two small pieces of masking tape

9. Glue

10. Art smock

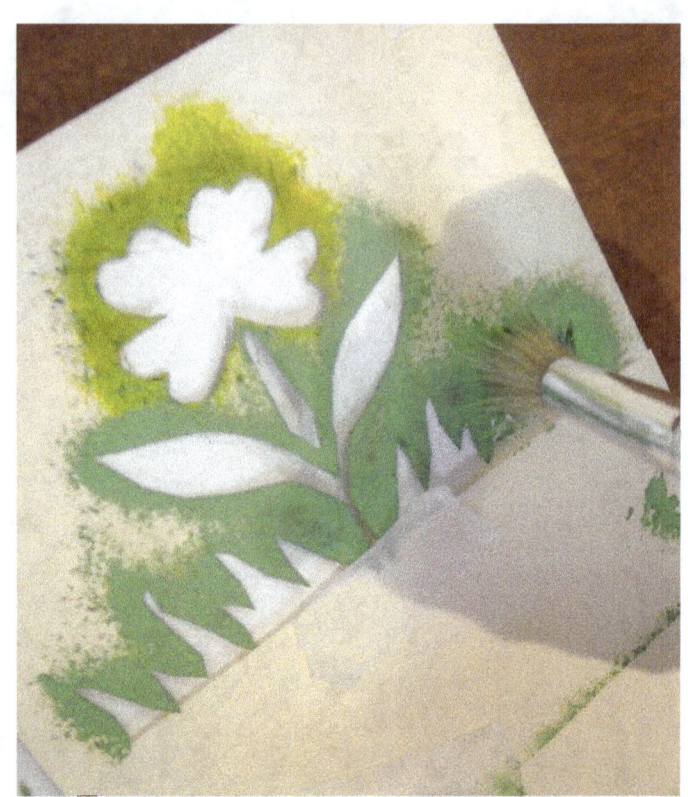

Supplies needed for instructor:

1. Easel with pad

2. Large black marker

3. 4" x 6" folded tag board

4. 9" x 11" piece of white construction paper

5. Scissors

6. Two stencil brushes

7. Squeeze bottle of red and green tempera paint

8. Bowl of water

9. Masking tape

10. smock

Before the participants arrive, follow the preparation rules of the art lesson on page 9.

Lesson

1. Introduce the word *stenciling and show an example.*

2. Demonstrate how to make half a tulip on the folded tag board and cut it out on the fold *(see image A below).*

3. Demonstrate how to tape the tulip stencil to the white paper *(see images B and C below).*

4. Place red and green *blobs* of tempera paint on the paper plate. Dip the first stencil brush into the red *blob* and tap off the excess paint onto the plate.

5. Stencil the tulip by *pouncing* the first stencil brush until the flower is filled in.

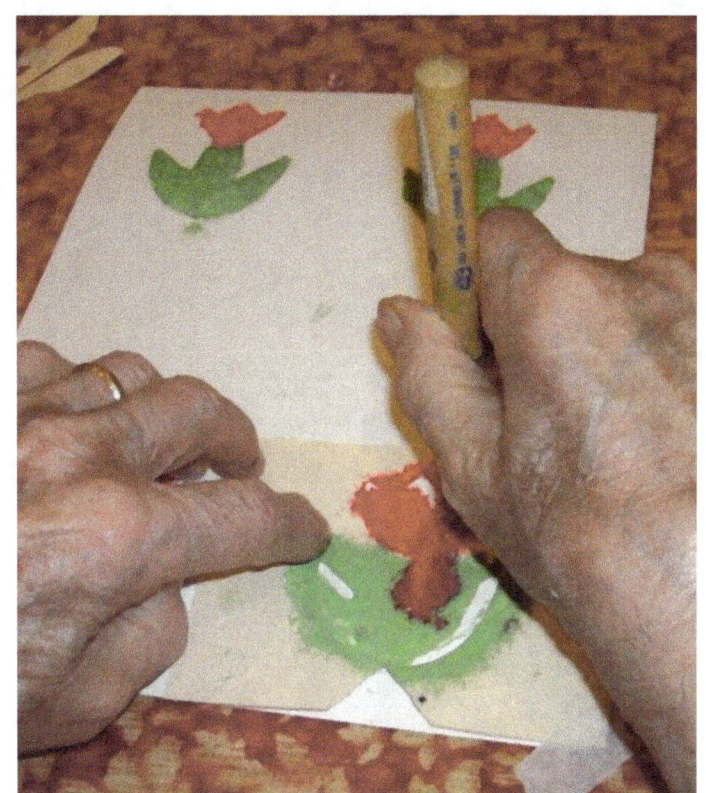

6. Using the second brush with the green paint, stencil the stem and leaf of the tulip green in the same manner.

7. Remove the stencil and display your finished stenciled tulip to the students.

8. Move the stencil and tape to another place on the paper and stencil another tulip the same way.

9. Have the students repeat the above stenciling procedure until their paper is filled.

10. When finished, have each student hold up their stenciled tulips and emphasize the fact that even though the same directions were given, each student's stenciled tulips are different because we are all individuals with different ideas.

11. Encourage the students to keep their stencil to make their own greeting cards.

12. Review the term *stencil* and tell the class that you will see them the next time in art class.

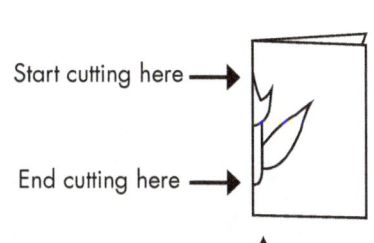

Start cutting here ➜

End cutting here ➜

A

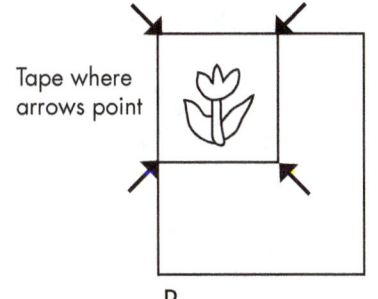

Tape where arrows point

B

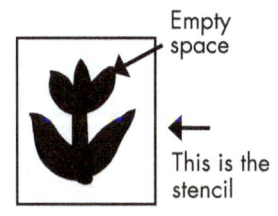

Empty space

This is the stencil

C

Bulletin Board Header

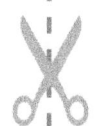

Stenciling

Stenciling is the art of cutting out a design or picture from a sheet of heavier material such as tagboard, plastic, or metal, and then transferring that picture or pattern to another surface such as paper, material, or glass by using a stencil brush and paint.

Symmetrical Quilt Block

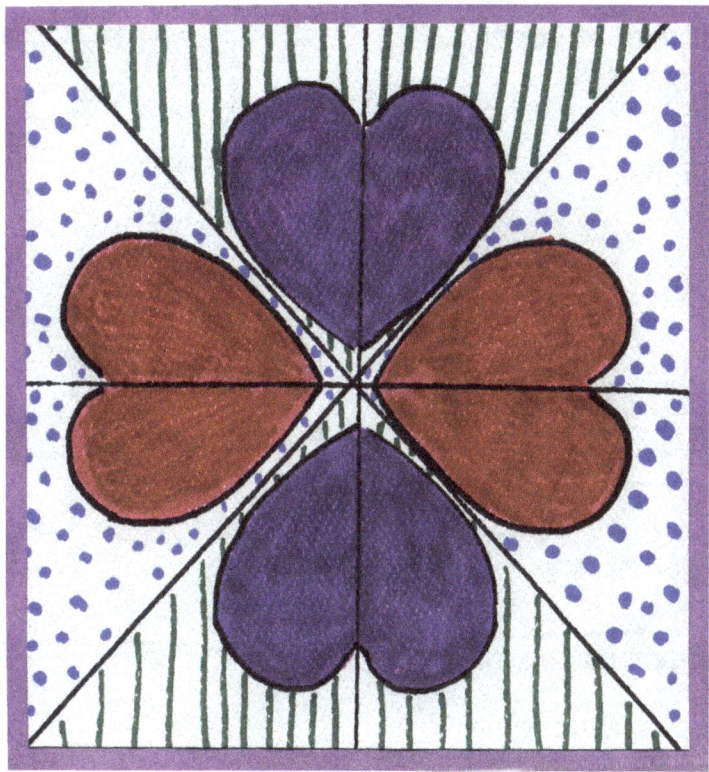

You can't get much more American than a good old fashioned quilt. We don't know for sure when people began to quilt, but it was probably a practical invention created out of economy and necessity. Traditional patchwork quilts are often made with shapes arranged into patterns called blocks. There are thousands of possibilities for creating patchwork blocks and many names for them such as Star of Bethlehem, Log Cabin and Bee on a Bear's Nose. Their patterns can be arranged symmetrically or in a happy hodge-podge of ideas known as a "crazy quilt."

Name of project: *Symmetrical quilt block*

Symmetrical is the term used to describe balance. In pure symmetry, identical objects are equally distributed in mirror-like repetition.

Objectives: To help the participants understand symmetrical balance by designing their own paper quilt square that transmits a personal, special message.

Getting started

Supplies needed for each participant:

1. 8" x 8" white square of paper

2. 3" x 3" square of tag board

3. Black Sharpie marker

4. Pencil

5. Scissors

6. Ruler or straight edge

7. 9" x 9" square of colored background paper

8. Colored pencils or markers

Supplies needed for instructor:

1. A small quilt or pictures of quilts

2. Floor easel with sketch pad

4. Large black marker

5. Roll of masking tape

6. A CD of instrumental music and CD player *(optional)*

Before the participants arrive, follow the preparation rules of the art lesson on page 9.

Lesson

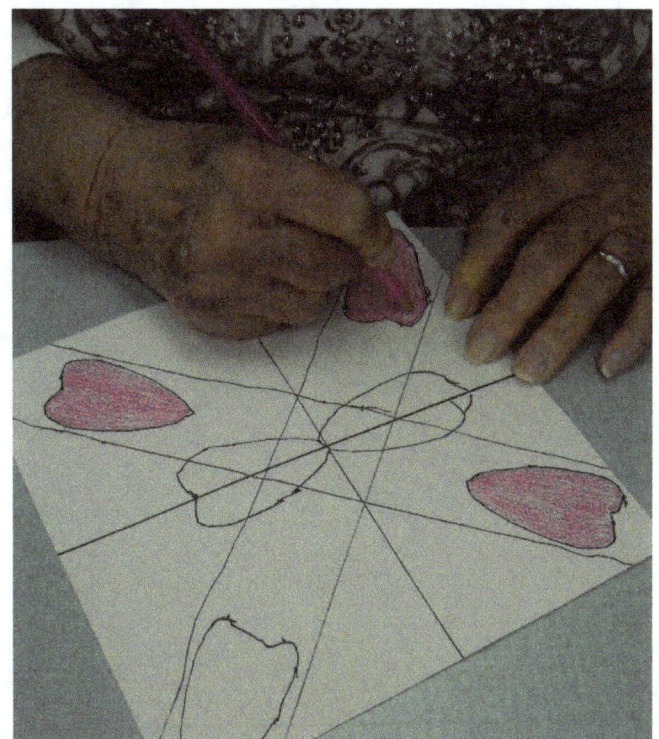

1. Introduce the brief history of the quilt to the class.

2. Demonstrate how to divide the 8" x 8" paper square into eight parts by setting the ruler diagonally from corner to corner and drawing vertical and horizontal lines *(see image A below)*.

3. Have the students fold the 3" x 3" tagboard squares in half and draw half a heart on the folded lines with their markers *(see image B below)*.

4. Next they should cut out the half-hearts and unfold them to make whole hearts.

5. Instruct the students to use the cutout hearts as patterns, trace the heart shapes onto the eight-section white papers, making sure the right and left sides are *symmetrical*.

6. Students should color designs with markers or colored pencils.

7. Finally, instruct them to glue their finished blocks onto the 9" x 9" colored background paper.

8. Write the name of each person on the bottom of their quilt blocks.

9. Display for all to see.

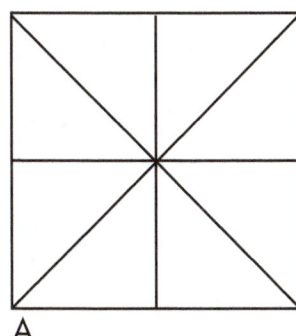

A

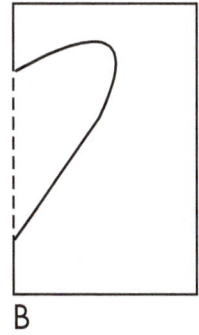

B

Bulletin Board Header

Duplicate page for multiple uses

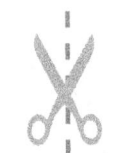

Block Quilt (Valentine)

You can't get much more American than a good old fashioned quilt. Each symmetrical heart quilt represents the care that your loved ones are sending to you for Valentine's Day.

Warm and Cool Colors

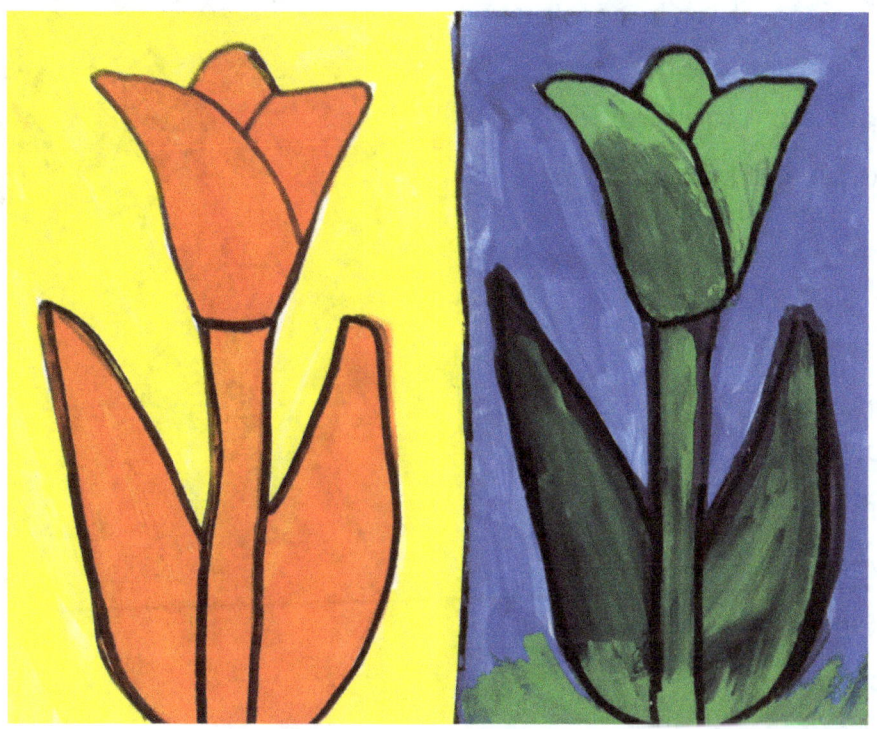

Colors on opposite sides of the color wheel give opposing feelings (*complimentary colors*.) The warm colors, reds, oranges and yellows, are often associated with fire and sun which suggest warmth. On the other side, cool colors, blues, greens and purples, are associated with water, sky and grass which suggest coolness.

Name of project: *Warm* and *cool* colors

Objective: to create a picture featuring warm and cool colors

Getting started

Supplies needed for each participant:

1. 8" x 11" piece of white construction paper
2. 4" x 6" piece of tagboard
3. Black sharpie marker
4. Scissors
5. Masking tape
6. Ruler or straight edge
7. Red, orange, yellow, blue, purple and green paint
8. #10 paint brush
9. Pan of water
10. Paper towel
11. Art smock

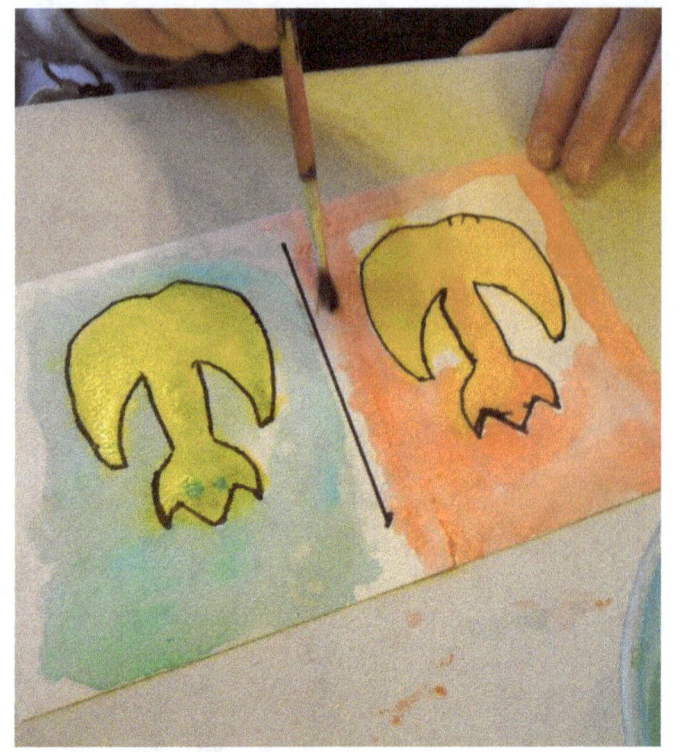

Supplies needed for instructor:

1. Visual examples of warm (the sun, fire, etc.) and cool (water, grass, etc.) colors
2. Floor easel with sketch pad
3. Large black marker
4. Scissors
5. 4" x 6" piece of tagboard
6. Ruler or straight edge
7. Red, yellow, orange, blue, green and purple tempera paint
8. #10 paint brush
9. Pan of water
10. Art smock or apron
11. Roll of masking tape
12. CD of instrumental music and CD player (optional)

Before the participants arrive, follow the preparation rules of the art lesson on page 9.

Lesson

1. Give a brief description of warm and cool colors and show examples such as the sun for warm and grass for cool. Ask the class to think of more examples of warm and cool colors.

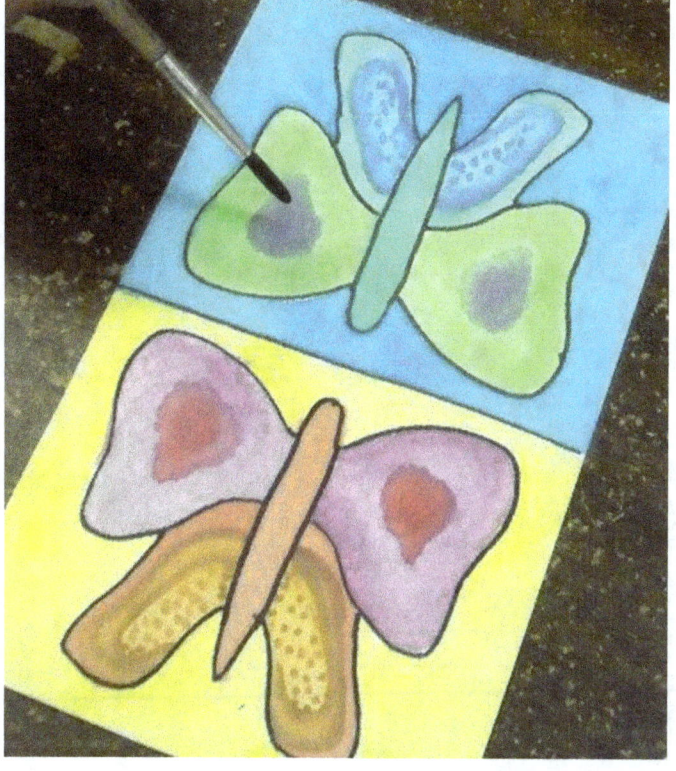

2. Fold your 4" x 6" piece of tagboard in half, and show the class how to draw half of a shape (e.g. heart, diamond, square, tulip, butterfly, etc.).

   Make sure when drawing that you start on the fold about a half an inch down and end on the fold about a half an inch up from the bottom.

3. Starting at the fold, cut out the shape keeping the tag board folded.

4. After cutting it out, open it and you will have a whole, "positive" shape. The remaining frame is called the "negative space."

5. Place the negative frame on your piece of white paper at the top left corner and trace all around it and in the inside. Repeat this to the right, or on the top if its vertical.

6. Explain to the class that they are going to paint one of the sections on their paper with warm colors and one with cool colors. Demonstrate with your two shapes.

7. Have the class begin by following the step by step instructions you demonstrated above.

8. When everyone is finished, show their work and display on a bulleting board for all to see.

*There are no mistakes in art,
just happy accidents*

Bulletin Board Header

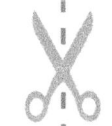

Warm and Cool Colors

Colors on opposite sides of the color wheel give opposing feelings. The warm colors, red and yellows, are often associated with fire and sun which suggest warmth. On the other side, cool colors, blues and greens, are often associated with water, sky and spring which suggest coolness.

Glossary of terms

Throughout this manual, many art terms and media are used. The following are simplified explanations and descriptions alphabetically listed to help you answer any questions that may occur.

Abstract art – art that is geometric in design or simplified from it's natural appearance; it does not have to look like anything real.

Action painting – a painting method(used by Jackson Pollock) that used movement to fling or throw paint onto the canvas

Art elements – components artists use to create, such as shape, texture, space, line and color

Art medium – materials used in creating an art work such as paint, crayon, paper, clay, etc.

Assemblage – an art process where three dimensional materials are jointed together to create an art work

Background – the part of an art picture the is farthest away from the viewer

Blob – a mass of shape or color create with ink or paint which has no particular shape but may look like something real.

Clay – an art material found in the earth

Collage – an art work created by cutting up materials such as paper, fabric, cardboard, photos, etc. and pulling them together with glue or other adhesives. Matisse is a good example of this kind of work.

Easel – a three legged stand used for holding paintings or large sketch pads.

Expression – when our inner emotions or strong feelings are shown through an art work

Free form shapes – shapes and forms with no geometric control; not regular

Graphic – a picture with a pictorial technique; more measured than interpreted

Horizon – when the sky and land seem to come together

Imagination – a human trait where we think up new ideas and make them into a work of art

Impasto – thickened paints applied to paper or canvas

Impressionistic – Showing an impression of reality rather than a perfect, life like report on the subject

Kiln – an oven used for baking clay which gets to a very high temperature

Landscape – a work of art where trees, mountains, rivers, sky and etc. ar the key features of a painting or drawing

Mosaic a work of art where bits and pieces of tile, paper, colored stone or glass are pressed into cement or are glued onto a surface (leaving a small crack.) As a result, a design or pattern are created.

Glossary of terms

Negative space – the space around and in between the chosen subject, drawing attention to the main subject's outline i.e optical illusion

Optical illusion – When the human eye and brain work together, an art work is created where things seem to move or appear to vibrate but are really not happening.

Palette – any type of board or tray where paints are mixed or chosen.

Pattern – an art work that is made when a design is repeated

Perspective – when an impression of distance and size are created in a painting or drawing

Pointillism – a style of painting where tiny dots of paint color are used instead of brush strokes. Georges Seurat was made famous by this style. By putting dots of color close together different shades of color were made. The closer the dots, the darker the color.

Pottery – containers such as pots, vases, or cups made from clay and baked in a kiln

Pouncing – an art technique used for transfering the outline of a design (stencil) from one surface to another using a stencil brush in an up and down motion

Proportion – the relation of one thing to another in respect to size, quantity and magnitude of corresponding parts, etc.

Primary colors – the three colors from which all other colors are made: red, yellow and blue

Realistic – showing life as it really is

Relief – a surface that has a raised up feeling when touched

Repetition – designs or patterns that recur over and over

Secondary colors – a secondary color is made by mixing two primary colors together i.e. red plus yellow (primary colors) makes orange (secondary color)

Sculpture – a three dimensional (height, width, and depth) art form that is usually freestanding

Seascape – water is the main subject such as the sea or ocean.

Silhouette – the outside shape of an object

Stencil – a thin sheet of material such as paper, plastic or tag board into which a design has been cut leaving a space to which a pigment is applied. A stencil can be used over and over for repetition.

Still life – arranging objects for the subject of a drawing or painting

Symmetry – when one half of something is exactly the same as the other half

Technique – the method used in creating i.e. crayon resist, impasto painting

Tempera paint – available in liquid or powder form, an art material used for painting pictures or objects

Glossary of terms

Tessellation – design that fit together perfectly in connecting designs; M.C Escher is famous for tessellations

Texture – the kind of surface in a work of art such as rough, smooth three dimensional (3D) height, width and depth are included in a solid art work such as a sculpture that stands up from a flat surface

Watercolor – a type of medium that is a thin, transparent water based paint found in watercolor boxes or squeeze tubes. When water is added to it, it thins out. The more water, the lighter the paint color. A darker paint color is made by adding less water.

Warm and Cool colors – colors on opposite sides of the color wheel giving opposing feelings. The warm colors (fire and the sun) are reds and yellows and the cool colors (water and sky) are blues and greens.

Definitions are taken from Wikpedia, and the book Discovering Great Artists *by Mary Ann Kohl and Kim Solga.*

*Freedom of expression is
art at its finest*

Janette Reineke

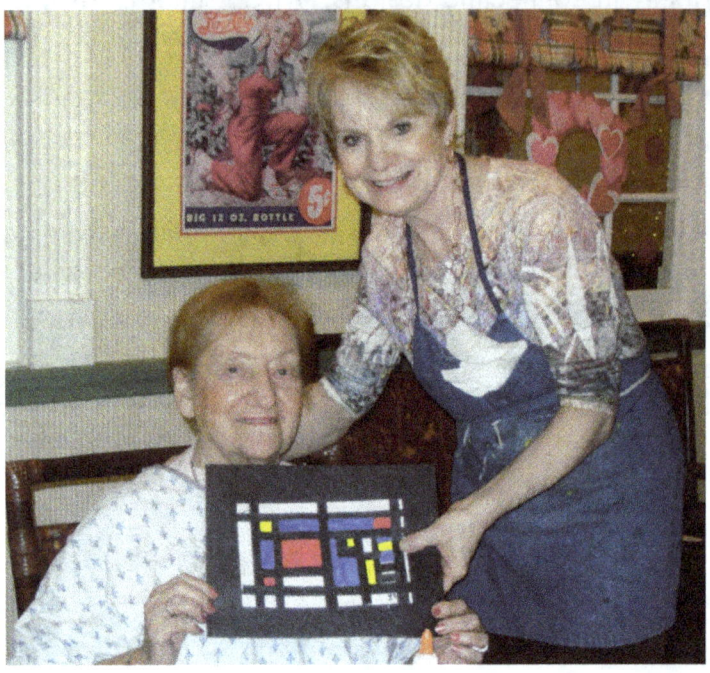

Janette received a BS in Education for grades K – 8 with a minor in art from Bluffton (OH) College in 1968. After teaching for 25 years in preschool, kindergarten, first grade, elementary and middle school art, she retired to continue her love of teaching art to the residents in nursing homes and assisted-living facilities. She occasionally offers workshops for children and private art tutoring.

[Left: Janette teaching Ida DiServio at Sunrise Senior Living Center in Findlay, Ohio. Used with permission.]

Acknowledgments

My deepest thanks and gratitude for the support of all the activity directors at the nursing homes and assisted living places and the residents who encouraged me with their love of art and helped make my "Young at H'art by Janette" art program such a success.

A special THANK YOU to one of my former art students, Alison King, graphic designer, who helped me develop and create this manual with her support and outstanding technical skills.

About the author